Make Your Way Across This Bridge

New & Selected Writings

Books by Patti Tana

How Odd This Ritual of Harmony (1981)

Ask the Dreamer Where Night Begins (1986)

The River (1990)

Wetlands (1993)

When the Light Falls Short of the Dream (1998)

Make Your Way Across This Bridge

New & Selected Writings

Patti Tana

Whittier Publications, Inc.

Published by Whittier Publications, Inc
64 Alabama Avenue
Island Park, New York
(516) 432-8120
800-897-TEXT
FAX (516) 889-0341

Copyright ©2003 by Patti Tana
All Rights Reserved.

ISBN 1-57604-162-X
Library of Congress Control Number: 2002117713

Acknowledgments begin on page 219

Cover photographs by John Renner
Cover design by Les Schacter

No part of this publications may be reproduced, stored in a retrieval system, or transmitted, in any form or by any means, electronic, mechanical, photocopying, recording, or otherwise, without the prior permission of the publisher.

Printed in the United States of America

10 9 8 7 6 5 4 3 2 1

*Last night
I dreamt a poet friend
built a bridge across a narrow
river — someone said Passaic —
more likely it was not
a waterway through earth
but a fluid passage —
my friend made a single path
with rope and slats and hand
over hand he pulled his way across*

*Today I have this dream
to lay across your path —
if you can, breathe in
whatever life surrounds you —
then as you let it out and out
      hand over hand
    hand over hand
make your way across this bridge*

For John and Jesse
    and my mother, Ada, who carried me
        across the country in a wicker basket
        and still holds me close

Thank you to my colleagues at Nassau Community College for sabbatical time to write this book, especially Professors Bruce Urquhart and Paul Doyle. I am grateful to Maxwell Corydon Wheat, Jr., for his generous editorial guidance; to Mary Gund for her creative ideas; to David Polinski of the Locust Valley Library for graciously teaching me how to use the computer; and to William Heyen for his inspiration.

CONTENTS

from *How Odd This Ritual of Harmony* (1981)
  Eros and Civilization 3
  Laughing Thoroughbreds 4
  Love Finds a Place 5
  Tropism 6
  We Touch by Accident 7
  The Turnkey 8
  Driving Across the Texas Night 9
  slender reed 10
  Crazed Mirrors 11
  Legacy for Louise 12
  Helen's Beauty 13
  Till Death Do Them Part 14
  How Odd This Ritual of Harmony 15
  Love Allows 16
  Torn Pictures 17
  Newborn 18
  The Line 19
  Summoned from Sleep 20
  Morning Warmth 21
  Father's Day 22
  Family Circle 23
  Cosmic Dancer 24
  Upon the Occasion of Your First Birthday 25
  Sweet Burden 26
  First Love 27
  Braiding 28
  Those Gypsy Eyes 29
  Talisman 30
  Dark Pages 31
  Stopped at a Light 32
  Still Life 33
  August 34
  Rosa Parks 35
  Long Beach, Long Island 36

from *Ask the Dreamer Where Night Begins* (1986)
   Down My Mother's Hall   39
   My Mother's Song   40
   Secret Passages   41
   Birds and Leaves   42
   Cat in a Dream Shop   43
   The Big Woman   44
   Possibilities of Pink   45
   You Like a Man   46
   Desire Followed Me Home   47
   Embarrassed by Dreams   48
   Snowbound   49
   I woke up   50
   Museum   51
   Piercing the Night   52
   That One Tree   53
   Men Against the Sky   54
   Sewing the Bullet Holes   55
   Go Gently Toward Death   57
   Raining Leaves   58
   I Am Your Witness   59
   Ask the Dreamer Where Night Begins   60
   The Lesson   61
   Missiles Cruise Toward Cuba   62
   The Window   63
   Clenched   64
   Invitation   65
   Vanishing Point   66
   The Words   67
   The Last Tear   69
   It Flies   70
   After He Left My Bed   71
   Still at Night   73
   Beware of Lovers   74
   Pause   75
   Tuesday   76
   White Cranes   77
   Wild Promises   78
   Garden   79
   Post Humus   80
      Coda: Living with a Poet   81

from **The River** (1990)
   The River 85
   A Brief Walk 87
   This Year 88
   Looking at the Fence 89
   No 90
   I have touched 91
   I Can't Believe the Moon 93
   Old Habits Die Hard: Milk 95
   Blind Trust 96
   White Space 97
   Tonight 98
   Western Window 99
   Streetlight 100

from **Wetlands** (1993)
   The Book of Clouds 103
   The Small Bed 104
   Subway 105
   Gifts 107
   Silver Dollars 108
   Found Money 109
   McKeever's Hill 110
   The Waters of Childhood 113
   Wetlands 115
   Makani 116
   Bread 117
   Harbor Island 118
   Stones 122
   Calling Up the Moon 123
   Natural Bridge 125
   No Guarantees 126
   Lineaments of Desire 127
   Marvelous Beast 129
   After the Flood 130
   Lucid Dream: Desert 131
   You Bring Me Back 133
   Seeds 134

The Wonders of Infinite Smallness   135
In the Doorway   137
For My Son Who Wants To Be Rich   138
Bequest   139
Palm Reading   141
Summer Storms   142
Touched by Zero   143
Weight   144
Threshold   145

from **When the Light Falls Short of the Dream** (1998)
Don't Slip Away   149
Fall Back   150
Late at Night   151
My Son's Shadow   152
The Nape of His Neck   153
Turning Fifty   154
Apples   155
Wild November Leaves   156
The Burning   157
The List of Names: Jean (1925-1995)   158
The Other Dream   159
Last Morning in Jerusalem   160
You Call from a Phone Booth   161
The Comfort of Time Zones   162
Seasons   163
The Guest   164
The Let-Down Response   165
Ginger   166
We Grew Up   167
The Hunter   168
Watching Him Handle Stones   169
If I Do Nothing   170
The Formation of Stars   171

New Poems: *Make Your Way Across This Bridge*

Mysteries
  Nothing Broke   175
  Fools Rush In   176
  Women Will Fall Open   177
  Mysteries   178
  The First Time   179
  Calling Out Your Name   180
  Turnings   181

Bruised Sky
  My Father's Coins   183
  Bruised Sky   184
  Silent Night   185
  Someone We Love   186
  Some Prayers Are Answered   187
  The Price   188
  Because   190

The Endless Horizon
  Intimacies   192
  A Sleeping Child   193
  Afterimage   194
  Moving Day   195
  The Endless Horizon   197
  Long Beach   198
  Notes to the New Owners   199
  Home   200
  Cabin Nights   201
  Night's Eye   202
  Smallwood   203
  Greedy 204

Index of Titles   207
Index of First Lines   213
Acknowledgments   219

from

How Odd This Ritual of Harmony

(1981)

Eros and Civilization

There he sat: Eros.
Here I sat: Civilization.

He wanted to seed;
I wanted to read.

After dialectical struggle
I decided to yield

my field to his plow.
When I satisfied

his need to breed,
I bred — he read.

Laughing Thoroughbreds

how many times
have I borne you
through the velvet night O
my thighs wrapped
tight O my thoroughbred

our small bed
vast space
where we birth
uncontrollable laughter O

my body
no longer woman
but silken flesh
on sinewy legs
galloping galloping

Love Finds a Place

Love finds a place
to live
some nearby park
or patch of ground
yielding
gnarled roots of an old tree
naked
from years of rain and
touch
even a doorway
the hard knob
nudging you forward
into each other's arms

wherever a stone bench
provides a seat
a porch glider
a hammock
the private cocoon
of even the smallest car
can be comfortable
in Love's
warm
moist
palm

anywhere there is space for two
there is space for one

first find Love
Love finds a place

Tropism

    speaking to you (my darling)
      while you sleep
        is like speaking to plants

    you turn toward my voice
      roots to water
        leaves to light

    my stroke awakens your skin

We Touch by Accident

We touch by accident
uncomfortable shiver
tug at caught hair

We touch by design
after reading between cold sheets
you enter me
            without transition
out of sync

Mornings you need black coffee
and newspaper
            I need you

The Turnkey

He shook the keys at me
the day he left home.
The sound of keys, even now,
jangles my bones.

That night, alone,
I found my diaphragm stolen.
That bastard!
He had to hold all the keys.

Driving Across the Texas Night

I placed the sleeping children
four logs
in the old station wagon
the night he tied me to the bed
and hurt me

then there was no thought
of the nights we heated the cold room
with our bodies — two logs
coddling the fire between our limbs

I dropped the diamond ring in an oil can
at the first station I stopped for gas

slender reed

              I awaken
to find myself swollen
like a pod
      invaded
         Suddenly
the hands of God
sweep me up
one holds me surely
the other squeezes down
the sheath of my body
till a tiny green speck
pops out and rolls away
as easy as a bead
slips from a broken string
a ring
from a sweaty finger

Then the hand
sets me down
once more
a slender reed

Crazed Mirrors

crazed mirrors
reflect shattered lines:

I will not be snagged
by the hem of my gown
in a mirrored door
I just slammed

I will not be left dangling
in the void between doors
glass doors closing
doors spinning faster
head twisting round&round
fingers clutch cracks
smear bloody circles
bright red circles
flash as I open the door
and scream

I will not be snagged
by the hem of my gown
in a mirrored door
I just slammed

Legacy for Louise

Just as they were about to be divorced
he died, leaving her minimum coverage,
a black top hat, and a son.

If spent with husbandry,
the money provides
essential food and rent.

The hat is tossed on a hallway peg —
collapsible vestige
of parties lost.

The son remains
a loud remembrance of why they wed
and the times she wished him dead.

Helen's Beauty

Born of feathered violence
sanctified rape
my beauty was a sword.
My hatch sister hacked and hacked
her daughter's murderer,
false father
who slaughtered his daughter
for wind.
Some women fled to caves,
shielded each other.
I stayed in the world of men
to spoil.
Ten years they killed
not for me
no
for gold, trade rights
honor justifying horror.
They split the remains
took women to other shores.
I went with my husband
convinced him I'd been stolen —
what matter this man's
or another's?
Now I am old.
My beauty has deepened
in reckless slashes,
my bitter revenge a shambles,
and I am content.

Till Death Do Them Part

He was going to leave, but fearing it
would break her heart
he never could.

She was going to leave
but never did;
she believed her vows forbid.

They were going to leave
but stayed instead
stayed and stayed until they were dead.

Now in their graves the two reside:
eternal bedmates   side by side.

How Odd This Ritual of Harmony

planting bulbs together in fall
knowing I'll be gone next spring
feeling the pain of causing pain
with each turn of earth praying
you'll grow to know
I leave to grow

how odd this ritual
of harmony with nature
growing and reaping
reaping and sowing
bulbs set in fall bloom in spring
gestating in earth like a child

the child you planted
died inside my womb
I wonder — would I be leaving
if that child took life
from us both
and bloomed

Love Allows

Love allows
a delicious selfishness
not permitted
solitaires

Lovers practice
the artistry of indulgence
elevating desire
to moral imperative

Like Michaelangelo's God
infusing Adam with life
my hand touches you
and we create life anew

Torn Pictures

I have not seen him since I was ten
but remember his face was big
with stubbled cheeks. Thick hairs
poked from his nose.
He was starting to bald
so he'd comb the strands back
over the space. I don't remember
his eyes or his smile, only his angry
stare and spit through clenched teeth
as he struck me.

I remember too the smell of house paint
he let me scratch off his face
in a moment of gentle holding.
But usually he smelled stale
from cigarettes and whiskey. Years later
when I would kiss a boy through sweaty fumes
of alcohol and tobacco, I would
think of my father.

When I was pregnant, I looked for his picture
in my mother's yellowed photographs.
I found ragged edges where he should have been
    his young bride, poised, smiling at no one,
    me as a baby suspended in my mother's arms —
    the other half of the bridge ripped away.
    Here and there remains his knee
    or his fingers

Newborn

Your face feeds at my breast.
One little Semitic face
selected from the millions.

The Line

When I conceived you
you marked me with a line
that spread down from my navel.

Darker with the growing months — a lifeline
trailing from the spot that showed I was born
to the place of your birth.

After you were born the line faded
and I was disappointed
when it disappeared.

Now pale stretch marks sign your first home
and your smile tugs the line
between your eyes and mine.

Summoned from Sleep

                Summoned from sleep
by the echo of your cry
I feed you from my body.
Your body, a thumbprint on my chest,
marks me with its rhythmic breath
as you melt back to sleep.

Morning Warmth

Awakening this morning
I find my child's body nestled
in my arms, head still
pillowed on my breast
from nightfeeding

In the fireplace
the tip of a log
warms the chilly dawn

Father's Day

Reaching for you this morning
across the breathing bundle, I let out
a small curse and think
our son has come between us.

I suppose it is a universal situation,
one of the archetypal patterns I must know
to be whole. Though it is a difficulty
the Holy Father never experienced with Mary.
He, after visiting her one night, left
her boyfriend Joseph to deal with morning
sickness and labor pains,
finding a safe dry place to nest
and all the rest.

Don't get me wrong. I know life
must yield to Life, but where
is it written we must forsake midnight
and morning embrace? And how
shall we increase and multiply at this rate?

So this Father's Day I offer
special thanks to that neglected step-
father who shared the family bed not just
with his child but with goats and ghosts,
dear father who ministered to the daily
needs of the real and fertile flesh.

Family Circle

Their glance defines my universe.
My son's blue eyes an ocean
reflecting the bright light
of his father's sky.

All day I hover in the ether
oscillating, ministering.
At night my body lies wedged
between their needs.

I steal time to write this:
I reel within the long drunkenness —
my life lacks ampleness —
before I sort out yesterdaytomorrow
is upon me.

No matter how tightly I stretch
the sheet will not tuck in
on all sides

Cosmic Dancer

The day you discover your fingers
you watch your hands glide like a dancer
through clear water

slowly you reach for a white blossom
gently you stroke the invisible breeze
beautifully you grasp your life

Upon the Occasion of Your First Birthday

Someday, my son, may you
Sleep in the arms of one who
Curls around your body —
Not a big C enclosing a little c
As I do now —
But a Great Sea against a Great Shore.
This and more I wish for you:
That she be warm and generous and gay
With wit to keep you dreaming
All night long
And well into the day.
For, son, you cannot stay inside my pouch
Forever
Nor do I wish to keep you in.
Frankly,
Your father's patience is wearing thin.
Many a night a brief hug or none at all
Has had to do in place of slow embrace
Because you came between.
He has made allowances,
But son, now that you are one
I think it's time you weaned,
So Dad and I can resume once more
A Great Sea pressing a Great Shore.

Sweet Burden

Carrying my child to bed tonight
I thought of all the times my mother
tucked me in to sleep with a blessing.
Sweet is the burden of cradling
an infant's head — how will we bear the old?

Mother, when you are old, let me
keep your hair brushed smooth, anoint your skin,
surround you with natural tones:
brown   green   blue.
And if I have to carry you
and clean and feed and bring you
roses on a tray, this burden would rest
like baby's breath upon my mother's breast.

First Love

How greenly the tree
and tall
she stood
growing toward the sky

She opened her arms
and I
climbed her
sure I'd fall
sure I'd fly

Braiding

when my hair was cut straight across my brow
and yours was pinned up on your head
the black still showing beneath the white

even then   in that gray girlhood
we leaned   toward one

even then   yours were the bright hands
braiding

Those Gypsy Eyes

Mother O Mother, it was so odd
The way you stared from the glass.
I shuddered at your knowing nod
And turned my glance away fast.

Mother Mother, bright were the eyes
Yet sadness shone there too.
Much though I loved those gypsy eyes
I did not want to be you.

Mother dear Mother, it took me years
To meet your gaze with gladness.
Now with a wink I quiet my fears
And welcome in the gladness.

Talisman

She who knows
the sunlit blush
on the bloom of the talisman rose
knows my mother.

Dark Pages

Curse you father
for making me hear doors closing
in the breath of the man who sleeps
beside me, dark pages turning
the noise of my son twisting in bed.
You lurk everywhere.
Dogs cannot bark you away.
The dawn brings only light relief.

I brace the gate
but still your footsteps creak on every stair
your eyes at my windows peer
your car comes closer
closer down an endless street

Stopped at a Light

Stopped at a light, I see my son's babysitter
step from her school bus and cross the street.
I am about to offer a ride when
the wind catches her hair
and the bright flurry catches my throat.

Her hair is the light brown color of my child's
— the low December sun fires it yellow and red
burning my eyes.

Then I notice a boy walks beside her
not holding her hand but pointing at something
and looking in the same direction.

I cry. Unaccountably I cry. Not the sobbing
heaves of sorrow, nor the dull moan of depression,
but a welling of memory denied
and wonderful confusion.

I pull into the station and pump my gas. This girl
halfway between my child's age and mine, poised
in that leap —

What else? I turn back and notice something
besides the hair — the jacket open (perhaps
winter will never come this year), the shoulders
back, the breasts comfortable on the chest (I,
still slouched from my childhood tallness, my early
prominences, my ill-fitting bras, notice).

And the scarf — not bandaged rounded her neck like mine —
tossed   flowing   her feet never touch the street.
The heath, the ease, the modest confidence.
I smile.
Driving home I remember my life is only half lived.

Still Life

Sharing a joke
we forget the daily death
the long wait in waiting rooms

For a moment there is
a bright flash on the dark canvas
and we draw together

The rest of the day we smile —
there is still life
still more life

August

All month long beneath a blistering sky
the shrill vibration of cicada swelled the air.

Today a lone bird cried, "Relief! Relief!"
And the sky threw down a light
tissue of rain
soothing the sore earth
making it beam with green gratitude.

Rosa Parks

kept wondering
what leads us to risk humiliation

kept thinking how revolutions begin
in an instant
that sets in motion infinitely expanding circles

kept superimposing on that giant moonleap
the image of your small step back
not taken

This keeping is for you, Rosa Parks,
one woman
with courage

Long Beach, Long Island

If this city were an island
not the illusion of island
I could test the limits of my home.
But beyond the channel, another island
mocks my isolation.

My island is a narrow finger poking the sea
joined to the body of land
rooted in the hard rock
cradling the illusion of ocean
contained in a cup of earth.

from

Ask the Dreamer Where Night Begins

(1986)

Down My Mother's Hall

Darkness down my mother's hall beckons
heart awake
I follow
stumbling against the walls
urged by the thrill of comfort

At last I rest engulfed
moist fur perfumes my body
large shapes yield to my touch
bad dreams drain from my night

My Mother's Song

We tied the line
>between strong trees
>>clear across the yard
I gave her pins
>one by one
>>as she gave me her song

Clothes caught the song
>billowed
>>and snapped against the sky
Leaves rustled the song
>and birds
>>tossed it like a bouquet

Now I sing a song
>a tall tree song
>>soft blue memory
wrapped in the clothes
>she washed and smoothed
>>and draped in the sky for me

Secret Passages

Between the legs of our property
a secret passage connected our yards.

In early summer
tendrils of honeysuckle twined the hedge
of our hiding place.

We waxed kite string with candles,
stretched through dense green,
punctured the bottom of paper cups
and knotted the string in the hole.

Through the heat of summer we burrowed
into cool earth
and drank voice to voice.

That was in another life.
We never speak. We never touch.

Only in early summer
the wet smell of honeysuckle
breathes its way into my body —
a sweet passage from an old song.

and Leaves

     s light
on my Japanese maple
matching the color of leaves.

Balanced on the branch
as only the living
rest upon the living,
birds and leaves.

       Then
fluttering for a moment
       leaves take flight

Cat in a Dream Shop

Tossed in a low bin of a dusty shop
a whimsical sculpture: one huge wheel
with spider web spokes and mustache handlebar.
Perched on the handlebar
a cat in a basket leaning forward.
The hand of a girl holds straight the wheel,
her long gown draping the roundness.
On top of her head, a circle of hat.

I wanted it for the sake of the cat,
the delicate spokes, the billowing gown,
the circle of hat and the wheel.
For I am that girl — full of surprise!
carrying cat in the bin.
The cat leans forward into the wind,
the sleek back curves like my gown,
the head is a circle with whiskers
flaring in feathery spokes.

I get on the wheel and ride in the wind —
a girl in a gown with a cat in the bin!

The Big Woman

The big woman settled down on the floor
a giant beanbag full
of purple green yellow blue
comfortable in her girth.

All night she sat there   a graceful boulder.
A big woman, I thought   a big happiness.

Possibilities of Pink

One day each year the earth cracks open.
Fiber by fiber
spring swells the rose.

Consider the possibilities of pink:
spring's blush deepens
quite naturally
magnolia's delicate veins
the spot on dogwood petals
the stunning flash of azalea.

Explore flesh: our folds
grow pinker
as they deepen the root of our bloom

  *   *   *

In my yard the weeping cherry
stands in rapture one week in April.

Earth breathes fragrance
fallen from trees of flowers.
When I hold my hand near
warm waves enfold me.

I open my hands and blossoms
fall to the earth.
The earth
is cushioned with blossoms

You Like a Man

You like a man's song
you like a man's smell
his gloves stay in your pockets
warming your thighs

You listen for his step
you listen for his call
his whistle enters your room
before he enters your door

You bring him your words
he handles them all tenderly
and gives you back your song

Desire Followed Me Home

Desire followed me home —
full moon on a spring night.
Desire stalked my steps —
white dog down a dark road.
Entering my door my room
I opened the shades and
moon burst through the window
pouring his light over my bed
licking my eyes my breasts
my hands my thighs
until I got my belly
full of rising moon
brilliant in the room

Embarrassed by Dreams

Embarrassed by dreams
I shook out the night
and tucked in the sheets.
              Pursued
by dreams, I folded
the shirt & gown,
covered the bed
cleared the breakfast
hung up the phone
and sat down to write
on a white sheet.

I peeled back the dark
layer of night   just
as we peeled off
the shirt, the gown
and the skin
of two purple plums
resting in bed.

Just this: one by one
touching
the delicate pulp
beneath the skin
moist softness
cushioning
a kindred softness.
              Just this.

Released by dreams
I folded the sheet,
the shirt, the gown,
and the plums
back into the dream
and tucked the dream
back into the night.

Snowbound

Inside the storm
      inside the warm room
   deep inside the heart's dream
      we are finger spelling
         in each other's hands.

For a timeless space
     there is no pushing away
as we draw close.
        In other rooms   the ordinary
      porcelain, garlic, linens.

Outside the air
    is starched white lace
binding us inside the warm
      room inside the song
        our fingers play

I woke up

kissing your neck.
Was it the storm outside or
the storm in my dream made me open
my eyes? I lowered my eyes
when you looked at me knowing
I came to your bed. Your look is kind
and cautious. Releasing a breath, petals
unfolding the fist of a flower,
I rest my head on your shoulder
as always, and now I am kissing
your neck. This time I'll not stop
with the skin of your beard,
this time I will moisten
everywhere lips and tongue
can touch beyond words.
Always the words did the touching and
now I will swallow your words
tender words the breath in the ear
will speak for us now
we are so close there's laughter
where my lips are touching
and lifting my eyes to see your lips
spread in a smile
I wake up kissing your neck

Museum

We are in a museum, alone.
The air crackles as we talk, as we touch.

Then we notice the pictures
looking at us.

A girl resting
her head in her hand, her arm on the table

now lifts her head and
definitely looks at us smiling.

Others turn our way as we hug
the corners of the room

softly lighted
the carpet thick as a mattress

and the sound of water
laughing in the fountain

Piercing the Night

we have warmed
fingers and toes
at each other's fire
nursing back from numbness
through pain

we have sat dark
watching words
burn their fiery path
bright arrows
piercing the night

and though we die
too soon
your words have been
shafts of light
warming the dark

That One Tree

When the storm blew down the tallest tree I could see
from my attic, wind tore roots from earth,
while apples, not quite red, dangled like Christmas balls
on a neighboring tree, their slender stems holding fast.

The man who came to cart away the tree called it wild
cherry, said the wood was hard, the tree old.

I never saw fruit or flower, but long I learned its shadow,
the changing shape it cast against the sky, the way its leaves
trembled, and morning sun would play through winter
bones.

One grand life rose above the houses.
That one tree was a forest.

Men Against the Sky

From my porch I see men walk against the sky
on wooden skeletons of new roofs.
Their hammers tell me
they're raising the horizon.

The sign foretold condominiums by September.
Here it is the fall and naked cement blocks squat,
blunt tokens in a monstrous Monopoly game,
on the last empty lot facing the boardwalk.

There's no pretending this delay means stopping
higher buildings, more expense,
for when I face the south I see
they're boarding up the sea.

Mornings I can still face east and watch the sun
filter through the spruce. By close of day,
when pollution from the city dyes the evening rose,
there's no escape — they're boarding up the sunset.

Even at night the clicking tracks
tap tap tap a warning:
one day we'll wake and find
they've boarded up the sky.

Sewing the Bullet Holes

When I finally could sew his damaged clothes,
I looked at the small hole in his heavy coat
then tossed it aside — amazed.
I decided to leave it that way, for luck.
The course threads of his burgundy sweater
seemed to reknit after the slug pushed through.
The shirt was creased and bloody, not torn,
so it must have been crumpled above his waist.

But the slacks required attention.
The bullet entered near the back seam of the waistband
and lodged under the skin at the base of the spine.
A cop pulled it out like a splinter
of shrapnel.
The doctors called it a miracle.

They were gray corduroy, worn soft.
The fiber in the back of the band was shredded
and a small tuft of wine-colored wool
was embedded in a dent in the stiff white buckram.
He wore no belt that day,
so merely the thickness of buckram
shifted the bullet's angle of entry
downward to a fabric more vulnerable
and kept the bullet near the surface of his flesh.

The white cotton nearest his body was stained.
My finger probed the hole and followed the route
over and over. The way I kept asking what happened
after they held the gun to your head?
What did you do?
What did they say?
What did you think?

Finally I threaded the needle
and stitched the gap closed.

It took longer for the scab to heal.
Now a shiny spot marks the wound, a glossy scar.
Now when he lies on me
and my hands reach around his back to press
his bulk against my crest,
I find the point of entry and gently rub.

My fingers search his flesh, feel the bullet,
then with a shudder
they pull it out.

Go Gently Toward Death

My arms cannot lift your dying
body, cannot ease the brutal
tearing.
                  Last night
I dreamt a poet friend
built a bridge across a narrow
river. Someone said Passaic.
More likely it was not
a waterway through earth
but a fluid passage. My friend made
a single path with rope and slats and
hand over hand he pulled his way across.

Just once he paused
to catch his breath
his breath was labored and that made me
think of you. And the tubes and straps
tying you against your will
were ropes across the water.

Yesterday you motioned for a knife
so you could cut your dying
body free of yellow
bags filling and emptying
and the strap   the strap
binding you to the hospital bed.
I could give you nothing.

Today I have this dream
to lay across your path.
If you can, please breathe in
whatever life surrounds you —
then as you let it out and out
              hand over hand
         hand over hand
make your way across this bridge

Raining Leaves

We are young together
my singing mother and I
raking leaves in our backyard.

She smiles down on me.
I leap in the pile and toss
them in the face of the sky.

Then I see her face grow old
through the raining leaves, withering,
her body shriveling into a shepherd's crook.

I jump up —
grab around her waist —
clutch her apron knot —

but she slips down   down
onto the waiting pile.
I look down and see leaves

I Am Your Witness

> *If you are my witnesses,*
> *I am the Lord;*
> *and if you are not my witnesses,*
> *I am not, as it were, the Lord.*
> —*Midrash*

Born in 1945
to finish the sentence of the dead
choked in the twisted throat
the silent cry
shoveled from the oven —
I am your witness.

Even before your survivors die
the killers deny your murder.

Though I never smelled the flesh
or sewed the star,
never screamed beneath the boot,
I dream of ovens exploding
yellow stars —
yellow stars looming into suns.

Born in 1945
between Europe's last gasp
and the first doomsday bomb —
I am your witness,
peddler on a ghastly street
carrying dreams of the dead.

Ask the Dreamer Where Night Begins

What is this period of time,
of blood?

As well ask the dreamer
where night begins.

I chase the sun
around the moving horizon

until I kiss my shadow
my daughter

and find
no distance, no time.

Through my body I have sent
a laugh into the world.

Will another be born to light,
or be shed like a tear
from the shelter of night?

The Lesson

When I reach the schoolyard
boys shooting baskets
run toward me
knock me down
spit on me.
A big boy with a cap
pees on me.

Our brothers teach us
we are spittoons
toilets
targets.

Just before death
Virginia Woolf writes,
"I still shiver with shame
at the memory of my half-brother
standing me on the ledge
exploring my private parts."

And my own brother —
flashlight in hand —
pulling down my blanket —

Missiles Cruise Toward Cuba

a small body of land
large enough to contain us all   Cuba
where sky and sea meet but not merge.

I call him and say Let's do it.
You've been urging me   Now
I say   Let's make love.
Let's roll our bodies into one body
large enough to contain us
all our life that will not become
our life
for the missiles are cruising toward Cuba.

That night we embrace in a dream
of an enormous ship containing everyone.
The blue outside might be sea or sky
I only know the journey
will last the night.

Come, I say   closer, closer
I want to feel the earth
beneath our merging bodies
within my emerging body
before missiles reach Cuba and all
merge in a bright flash: sky land sea

Though I dream I am dreaming of missiles
gently piercing a sandy shore
that night he does not enter me

but every night thereafter
                missiles cruise toward Cuba

The Window

She opens the window;
he closes it.
She sticks with sweat;
he feels no heat.

She wants to scream
and strike his face —
the window — the sky —
but brings his pillow
and offers him tea.

He fingers the surface of cloth
looking for threads.
Sometimes
his hands flutter from his body.
When she speaks to him
his thoughts scatter —
sandpipers
before the rim of the wave.

Inside the walls seem to heave
with labored breath. Outside
the sun has bleached the sky
white

Clenched

I help him match his morning tie.
I marinate his steak in ginger and tamari.
I rub oil between his toes.
Yet he turns from me.

When he returns he wants me
thinner, more stylish.
My lover, my Shylock,
demands pounds of flesh before he strokes me.

I eat myself fat with desire
while he pinches my skin between his fingers.
How tight must I keep my stomach clenched?
Soon I will turn my hind parts to his face.

Invitation

Nights he sleeps away from home
I practice sleeping alone
knowing the night will come
when the dark challenge falls.

I check all locks a second time
even the flimsy latches.
Metal bars line ground floor windows.
Flood lights shine.
The dog has finally learned to bark.

Tonight in my aloneness I write
> *Old friends, join me*
> *with records, photographs,*
> *new songs and poems. Nourish me.*
> *Be with me in my home*
> *new to me in its emptiness*
> *and help me feel safe.*

Vanishing Point

It is easy to leave
again. Each time you threaten
(brows pursed above a dark glance)
I dance one step back,
two to the side.

It is important to keep smiling,
to fix the eyes surely
on the sunset, the dish, the picture —
whatever provides harbor.

But especially the sunset:
Notice how it flattens along the horizon
then swiftly swallows itself,
the last drop of gold becoming
the first night star.

It is so hard to let go the first time
but easy to leave again.
Books reside on separate shelves,
records are divided.
My heart, too, has been rent

part remains, smiling next to you,
part is in a country washed clean by tears
where I live without your threat.

Watch how easy it is to leave.
Just keep threatening
and watch me
vanish

The Words

And at the end   the words
held us together
talking through the night
the dear sounds
carried us across the country
across the years
to our joining. Our words
appeared like stars
spelling the names
we named ourselves.

On the eve of our divorce
I sat alone in a dark concert hall
listening to poets trying to stop
the end of the world with words.
All I could think of was the night
before we gave birth
holding hands in a concert hall
water dripping onto the floor.

After his birth
and after you went home exhausted
from helping my body let go
of our gift
I lay still in a dark room
my hand gripping the phone
your voice pouring happy happy
into my ears   for years
for years the sound of your voice
lit the room and hummed in my body.

At the break
I hurried from the poets' hall
hurried to the train
water dripping on my face
hurried home to our last night.

And at the end   the words
loosened my grip on your hand
and helped me let go

The Last Tear

I will wear black
   my feet slippered in slow step
      my arms waving lonely! lonely!

I will drape sad mirrors with white sheets
   sit on a crate made of wood
      smear my body with ashes.

I will rip my clothes and rise naked
   drench my skin in the sea
      flush my pores clean of his scent.

And when I cry the last tear I will catch it
   and place it high in my east window
      so every dawn will splash the day!

It Flies

From my porch
I hear birds call and answer
in random joy.

Then I notice a lone bird
drawing its wings to its body
like gills breathing

as it flies.
Without understanding how it flies
it flies

After He Left My Bed

   After he left my bed
sex hung on my body, a heavy coin
dangling from my ear
jangling each time I moved my head.
He had taken my feathers and beads,
he had taken my hey! high laugh
and my loose long gown.
But I still had this gold coin.

   Looking in the mirror
I thought of the gold pin
piercing the lobe of slaves.
And I had been a slave of desire
lashed to that pole. Our naked bed
an agony of desire
knowing he entered another.

   When my bed was empty
my body curled into itself.
The thought of someone inside me
closed me like mimosa
shut against rude probes. The men,
the men with their foolish lips,
puckered word sounds —
eying my gold piece.

   What were they whispering?
My ears closed. I heard nothing.
I felt nothing.

   So I determined to rescue pleasure,
simple friendly passion, whimsy,
anything but love. My body would be
an instrument of pleasure.
No man would put his mark on me.

      Testing myself, I chose a sailor
who knew the stars, the wind,
knew how to hold a boat on high seas
leaving only foam in his wake.
And I would guide him into me naturally
— a fish fluttering downstream.

      When he came to me in my home, worthy
and whole, I unpinned my gold earring
from the fleshy place it had hung so long
and cast it in the sea
the way Li Po cast poems into the river.

      After he left my bed, I slept well
that night. But the next day I could not eat.
My body opened and emptied of reason.
Nothing would hold inside me.

      Now I pace inside my home
curious to learn the stars.
And when I step outside, the wind
blows songs through the cords of my body.

Still at Night

Still at night
and bright afternoons
I miss your body
that formed with mine
one body
shaping and reshaping
warming one side
then the other.

I have learned to sleep
alone. The fear I feared
would kill me
has not.
I can relieve my body's
manufactured ache.
I have let men
rest beside me
in your place

but I am learning
the limits of the flesh
to warm the soul.

Beware of Lovers

I wanted hardness when I met him.
To be taken on the hard wood floor.
To see his hard mask soften.
To soften my hard longing.

But nothing in me wanted the hardness of the knife.

The lover I was seeking
became the stranger creeping to my bed.

Now I am humbled. I am just like anyone
who swims beyond the force of arms
swept by strong currents.

Now I am never more than a knife edge
from fear.

A new character stalks my dreams.
Rape has a name and a face: Fear
sits at the bottom of my bed chanting

Beware of lovers.
Beware of lovers who are strangers in your bed.

Pause

There are times I pause
at the bottom of the stairs
to note how well a chair fills a corner.

                         Mushrooms
spring from the empty lot next door
after a wet night.
                 The sea replenishes
the beach with broken shells. Shapes, colors
tempt me to hold them
before they are ground to sand.

And most amazing: bones reknit
with only a forecaster's twinge to re-
member the fall. Flesh smooths a raw sore.
In due season the eye regains its luster.

It's in the pause that I glimpse the healing.

Tuesday

I drove my son to school so he could stay warm
a little longer. Soft wet snow began to fall.
When we rounded the corner he looked for the buses
leaving clusters of children, and glad he was not late
sat back against the seat.

A crossing guard stamped snow dust from her feet,
her full curly hair dotted with flakes, and he said
that would make a good poem.

When I arrived on campus, students were hurrying
to class. Snow continued in a steady silent fall.
Then I noticed a flock of geese on the lawn.
All day I looked to see if they were still there
and they were.

Between classes I moved a chair to my office window,
raised the shade, and watched the pattern
of snow against dark branches.
The constant movement made me calm. I wrote,
the motion of snow / the wisdom of geese

All day I missed him at school.
Tuesday night I dreamed about a small house by a river.

Wednesday morning my son ran for his school bus
and I walked the dog. The night rain
had made thick slushy puddles of yesterday's snow.

I thought — when he leaves there will be
the motion of snow
the wisdom of geese
and the comings and goings of school children
watched by the crossing guard

White Cranes

One white crane lifts from the field
    another follows — awkwardly —
        and steadies into a long stick

Up they soar — graceful dashes —
    one slightly beyond the other — then lock

The coupling cranes glide above the earth —
    marking the sky

This dream flies three times
    I fly with them
        feel the ease of joining

When I wake I find
    a long white feather in my bed

I lift the feather from the sheet
    and write of two white cranes —
        two elegant gestures

Wild Promises

I open my book
    and words blossom into wild promises
        colors leap from black and white

Who is she? How can she be
    so fearfully unafraid? Some fool
        might light his match on her flame

She opens her hands   land without boundary

Dare I enter the purple ripening
    trees thick with fruit
        rice sprouts between my toes in wet fields

Wings rush my face as I touch
    speckled eggs resting in straw —
        nights I ride the red sky and bite the stars!

When she opens her mouth
    the tongue of morning
        licks the faces of contented sleepers

I open my eyes
    and she hands me a bouquet:
        wild promises grow from her fingers

Garden

It is May and I am
drowsing in my garden
where everything is a kiss —
bees sample the yellow tips
of flowering tongues,
the breeze fumbles large green leaves,
quiet bells tremble.
A bird thrusts its song into the garden —
a shadow flies

Post Humus

Scatter my ashes in my garden
so I can be near my loves.
Say a few honest words,
sing a gentle song,
join hands in a circle of flesh.
Please tell some stories
about me making you laugh.
I love to make you laugh.

When I've had time to settle
and green gathers into buds,
remember I love blossoms
bursting in spring.
As the season ripens
remember my persistent passion.

And if you come in my garden
on an August afternoon,
pluck a bright red globe,
let juice run down your chin
and the seeds stick to your cheek.

When I'm dead I want folks to smile
and say, "That Patti, she sure is
some tomato!"

Coda

Living with a Poet

I open my mouth to speak —
you place a poem on my tongue.
They fall from you
even as you sleep — especially as you sleep.
Mornings I get out of bed
and crush them on my way to the bathroom.

Your words stain my sole.
I soak and scrub but cannot wash them off.
They stick under my fingernails
when I scratch your scalp.
They flash on my eyes
when the sun filters through my lids.

I see myself in them — distorted
in a fun house mirror
or partial, as bits of glass
sewn on a bright robe
reflect here a lip, there a patch of skin.

They do not show me whole.
They do not show me soothing
your raw pain
before it is tame enough to pen.
They do not show me bleed
when you slice part of me for public show.

You offer them to me, proud
as a girl in communion dress.
Forgive me if I gag upon the truth.
I would keep private our confessions.
You hold them out before you — candles
lighting a dark passage.

from

The River

(1990)

The River

All the bright day I rode my bike along the river
gold flashing among the dizzy leaves
water clear and rushing over stones
the sound drawing me on.

All day I rode with the wind in my face
till I lost a shoe when I drank at the river
and turned to go home.

It was dusk when I entered the old
house on the hill
and you were glad to see me.

You showed me strings you had tied to a stick.
I watched you dip strings in hot tallow
again and again
while the long tapered bodies grew thick.

Then you lit two of your candles
and there in the flickering shadows we stood
between floors on a landing.
You reached to embrace me as I turned toward you

and gently your lips brushed on my lips
and gently your tongue entered my mouth
finding the way through the dark

I stood open — river swelling inside me —
rising and falling —
walls breathing for me —

the sound of the river rushed in my ears
my legs were water (I might have fallen
if your arms had not held me)

Finally
you turned with a smile as though it were natural
and walked down the stairs,
leaving me filled
with that long trembling.

When I could speak I said *Let's walk by the river.*
Then I asked *Will you be loving?*
and laughed at my words.
I meant to say, Will you be leaving?
and then you laughed too.

A slip of the tongue, you said.
Yes, I said, *a slip of the tongue.*

A Brief Walk

We had time only for a brief walk
long enough to hear the water
moving swiftly over stones —
their bald domes rising from the shallows.

Near the river I found one that fit in my hand,
smooth and dry, split in two.
Inside were dark shapes —
            two halves of a moist heart.

This Year

let's shake loose the fall
upon our faces
and if it rains
the rain upon our faces.

Let's get lost
with the map in our pocket
and thunder
rumbling our names.

For now I will measure by seasons
my time on the earth: this fall
giving way to winter
till winter sun melts the snow
and swells a mountain spring
where lions come to drink.

Looking at the Fence

*We should have stayed
looking at the fence* he said
after we drove to the open
bay where apparently random stakes
made patterns in the water.
No gulls perched on the pole
as they did in his memory
but a narrow stick turned
in the wind on top of one.

Spotlights from the pier
seemed to feature the wind
stick and focused our attention
on that spot of light within
a cloudy dusk. Something
in the shape of the dark
hills beyond that he had not
photographed when he lived there
and that one windy spot of light
undid him.

I miss the birds he said
and something about a child's
toy, then hurriedly drove us away.

No

I will not speak
when words stick in my throat like bricks,
when all words say *love me*
love me as I love you.

I will not speak
when I am feeling like a wall of bricks
that runs along the bottom of a hill
where water seeps.

Touching the wall
moss springs green and soft and moist
and silent as the first forest after rain
before birds learned to sing.

No, I will not speak
when I would rather touch.

I have touched

your hair
with the palms
of my hands
I have fingered
the strands
around and around

your ears
with my words
I have tickled
with laughter

your neck
with my tongue
with my teeth
with my lips
I have kissed

your thighs
with my thighs
pressing between
ha! I have touched

your feet
your scars
you said you bleed hard
as I traced the soft flesh

your hands
with my hands
your chest
with my chest
and even your heart   yes!
especially your heart

my cheek to your breast
as it rises and falls
my breath in your hair
the wind in the leaves

oh yes these
I have touched

I Can't Believe the Moon

I can't believe the moon
that hangs above my house
(an empty bowl
slightly tipped)
also hangs above your house.

I understand the turning of the earth
brings sun to you an hour late,
how forecasters say
the whole country will be sunny
— sunlight blazes far away and so immense.

But the moon, the moon appears
shyly from the sea
and shuttles westward through the dark —
a private code to those who know
the patterns of replenishment
and loss.

Last full moon I awoke to the vision
of my room filled with bright shadows
filtered through curtains.
Reaching out my hand I touched the lace
the moon had cast upon your skin.

I keep track of three stars you taught me
form Orion's belt.
When I looked to the end of your pointing finger
(your other arm around my shoulder)
they were just above my yard.
But now they too have traveled west. I fear
I'll lose them soon.

For now it seems everything turns west.
My eyes follow the dropping sun.
And though you're just an hour away
reckoned by the sun,
I can't believe the moon
shines through your bedroom window
as it shines through mine —
          moonlace on your skin.

Old Habits Die Hard: Milk

the way I keep shaking the milk
long after the cream is mixed by machine
long after I started drinking milk
without cream —
pale drops splatter when the seal is broken

the way the cat keeps leaping on the screen
clinging white belly and eyes
long after my neighbor said
stop feeding it

the way I keep reaching for the phone
to lap up your voice
long after you've gone
long after you've gone

Blind Trust

one day we took turns
feeling what the blind could
not see
being led through
doors I never knew existed

the sound of you becoming
the physical world
words the shape
of things and spaces

out on the grassy field
the shower of sun was blood
on my eyelids and the earth
solid   giving   dark
rose with each step
through me

with you away
distant voices return
laughing familiar
in a fabric of conversations
taking apart the spaces

and in dreams you
turn   nearly maternal
parting the tender folds
your blind eye
finding the red darkness

White Space

knowing you need to be
in your immediate distance
I explore white space

profile
                 shadow
    aura

imagining the unseen
embracing the intangible
this gift of contradictions

speaking to you
even when I can not
speak with you

Tonight

I conjured up your image
for the first time in months.
You were home
but not one I recognize —
carved in the side of a mountain
with ivy on rock outcrops
in your backyard where you were fixing me
breakfast. I stopped your busyness to beg
you to be comfortable with me,
not to waste the little time we had.
And you asked, *If you had to choose,
what would you choose?*
And I answered, *To be understood.*
Ah, that you have, you said,
your eyes steady in mine.

Then you were sitting on the floor
in the middle of a room
with a huge dictionary open before you.
We seemed to be in a hospital ward —
narrow metal beds with thin covers
and a woman in white behind a glass wall.
You were looking up the word "inclination"
and we were playing
with the meanings. I tried to convey
how it feels to know the outcome of a fall
at the moment of descent
everything shattering before me and
nothing I can do to stop it.
And you said, *So,
you understand.* And I said, *Yes.*

Western Window

When a new house blocked the trees
I broke through the bedroom wall
and moved my bed west.

Outside the west window
bare gray branches of maple
pointed all directions.

Through his crazy lattice, two blue spruce
traced the wind with symmetrical limbs,
gold cones dangling in the sun.

And beyond the spruce, the daily show
of clouds and birds and planes
across the shades of sky.

It is spring now, the first
spring through my window. Buds
nipple the branch, then flare.

Yesterday a strong wind sent blossoms
flying and today I can almost touch
the unfolding leaves.

Streetlight

I'd forgotten the streetlight, forgotten
roofs and flat sides of buildings beyond
the curtain formed by the maple.
A strong wind blew all but a few faded leaves
from quaking branches.

Now a light shines through my window,
one sharp point of light
beyond the dark shapes
before the greater darkness.

from

Wetlands

(1993)

The Book of Clouds

Next to my mother's bed she kept
a small book of clouds.
Printed on the dark blue cover
in gold letters
was my brother's name.

He was much older than I, a special
guest in white sailor suit, handsome
and smiling an official smile.
I knew him only well enough
to adore him.

When he came home we would dance
The Princess Waltz, my feet on top of his,
soles lifted from below,
arms stretched up   up
beyond his long legs to the real smile.

And when he was away I had
the book of clouds, magic words
in bold face letters
below hazy forms: **cirrus, stratus,
cumulonimbus.**

Resting at her bedside
his name — my name —
brought word from a world beyond
the big bed down the hall where
my father made my mother cry.

The Small Bed

In the small bed
in a room made out of tin
I slept.
        When the rain beat sudden
drums on the roof
        I dreamed.

And when the house was too quiet
when the angry echoes were still
I cried —
        my pillow a raft on the night.

Subway

He sees the long legs and the trim
along the edge of her
collar, and thinks a man
could make a go of it
with a woman like that

She feels someone watching
and lays a ribbon across the page
to hold her place
and looks up at the near man
swaying with the motion of the train

He sees her brown eyes and the fine
line of her lip
and he wants that face
to smile at him
and he wants to start again

She looks down to the book in her lap
still seeing the brim of his hat
tipped back
and thinks how foolish she is to want
to go dancing
instead of home from work

As the train approaches her station
she rises from the seat, and the stop
jolts their bodies together
long enough for them to fumble
apologies giving him the chance
to walk her to her father's apartment

By the time the little girl is born
love is long buried beneath his lies
and she is just another
new start that fails

All her wit and all her will
could not move them from the track
they rode

But there is another story
about a daughter
who learned from the mother to love
long after the man is gone

Gifts

The first holiday after the divorce, Jack sent us gifts. It was strange and scary because my father had never given us anything. Never played games or made things with us or sang us a song. We lived in a minefield. No matter how careful we were, he'd explode.

We weren't sure if we should accept the gifts, but we didn't know how to send them back. My little brother played the drums with savage insistence, and then his jazz rhythms became the background music of the house. My big brother didn't know how to work the hand brake on the racing bike, so he crashed into a parked car on his first ride. The doctor wrapped his ribs with wide strips of tape. The gift Jack sent me that holiday is not only lost but forgotten.

About six months later though, I did have a dream about a crate of oranges from Florida. Fat bright fruit that smelled like blossoms. Attached with wire to the wood slats of the crate was a tag addressed to me from him. Later that day a man stopped my older brother as he left school and told him that Jack was living in Florida and that he was sending us a crate of oranges.

We never received oranges or anything else from him. Never saw or heard from him again. But I still have dreams of the long shadow Jack cast down our narrow hallway where he threatened to kill us if my mother divorced him and of his car following me down an endless street.

I used to have dreams born of the terrible longing for a father's love. The night before my commencement speech, Jack stood in the back of the auditorium, radiant with pride. But when I gave my speech, he was not there.

The night before my wedding I dreamed that Jack came to see me in the temple. I stood at the altar and he stood in the doorway. He held no gifts. He gave no blessing. We looked at each other and said nothing. He did not ask for forgiveness, nor did I offer it.

Silver Dollars

We were poor, but never broke. Hidden beneath the shoes in my mother's closet was a black pocketbook full of silver dollars that she saved from the tips she earned as a waitress. When she came home from work, she'd empty all the coins from the big pockets of her apron onto the kitchen table and I'd help her sort and stuff them into wrappers of faded red, blue, green, and orange.

About once a month Mom would bring home a silver dollar. On my favorite one the eagle's wings are folded and PEACE is written on the mound where it perches. On the other side of the coin is the head of Liberty crowned with rays, her hair flowing back from her face.

The dollars were round and solid and heavy, made of real silver, and they seemed to be worth much more than green paper that creased and soiled and tore. The most I counted was one hundred and fifty. When they ran low, I became nervous. Usually the bag contained about one hundred dollars, and that was enough. I knew we could dip into the stash and buy a quart of milk, a dozen eggs, and a large loaf of seeded rye bread for one silver dollar.

One time when I had my heart set on going to the movies I was disappointed that my mother didn't have enough money. Admission was twenty cents, the same as a quart of milk. She thought for a minute, smiled, and went upstairs to her room. When she came down she placed a silver dollar in my hand.

"No," I protested, trying to give it back to her. "They're only for emergencies — for necessities — "

"This is a necessity," she assured me. "The soul needs sweets."

I knew what she meant. She'd often told the story about her father, her beloved Papa. It was the Depression. She was raising her first child alone, with whatever help her father could give her. They were shopping in a crowded grocery store when a young woman placed her selections on the counter, including a small carrot cake. Quietly she asked the clerk if she could pay the bill at the end of the week when she was paid for her work.

"No cake for beggars!" he boomed, putting the cake back on the shelf. Everyone was stunned into silence.

Then Papa said, "Give her the cake. The soul needs sweets."

I took the silver dollar and went to the movies. I even bought a chocolate bar with almonds to eat during the show.

Found Money

Almost every day I find
a penny on the street.
And if the penny faces up
I call it luck.
And if it's down
I call it money.

When I was young I helped my mom
clean a store at night after her regular job.
I'd spray counters with ammonia
that went up my nose and stung my eyes
then rub away the fingerprints with a cloth.
I'd scrape gum from the floors
and hold the pan as she swept in dirt.

Sometimes I'd find coins in the dressing room.
I even found a dollar behind a row of gowns.
No matter if I found a dollar or a dime
Mom made me leave it with a note
on the big wooden register.

Once I found a wallet
on the floor of the movie theater.
No name. No pictures. Only money.
Even in the dark I could see
it was red, smooth plastic red.
I looked at my mother
and she looked away.

Almost every day I find
a penny on the street.
And if the penny faces up
I call it luck.
And if it's down
    I call it money.

McKeever's Hill

Behind our house on Simpson Place
where I grew up, an empty lot rose steeply
to Smith Street. From the kitchen I could see
the rise of the raspberry patch at the back
of our yard, then the hedge that marked
where our property ended and
McKeever's hill began.

McKeever must have lived
in one of the big houses flanking the hill.
Or maybe he owned the place across the street
from the hilltop before it became
Nardone's Funeral Home.

The spring I learned to walk
Mother watched in the yard as I tested
my legs on the small mound near the berries.
Again and again I'd make my way up
and then run down, laughing
even when I fell.

Coming home from school I'd gallop down
McKeever's hill or stretch out sidelong
tumbling earth,sky,earth,sky,earth,sky
like a rolling pin on a tilted table.
No one ever shouted or shook an angry fist.
No one ever pulled aside a curtain, scowling
and rapped on the glass.
No one ever stopped me.

In the gathering shadows of summer evenings
kids played kick-the-can in front of my house.
We could hide behind the houses, but McKeever's
was out of bounds. After play we'd plead for coins
to buy ice cream at the store beyond
the funeral home.

Much larger than a house, stark white
with black around enormous windows,
Nardone's Funeral Home had wide stone steps
leading up to carefully tended gardens.
We'd dare each other to peer through the lace
at the men in dark suits. Still more daring was
a peek into the cellar that smelled like a hospital.
We'd scrape our feet on the gravel driveway
but when black limousines lined the way
we'd sneak by.

Hands full of ice cream, we retraced our path
through the funeral grounds, down the stone steps,
across the street to McKeever's hill shouting
"Race you to the bottom!" and gulped down
the last bit of melting ice cream,
tossing away the stick.

On snowy winter days, children with sleds were safe
on the hill from cars skidding on icy roads.
I'd sit up and steer with my feet
on the wood crosspiece, the rope in my hands.
Or feeling brave I'd lie on my belly gripping
the bar, chips of snow whizzing by,
spraying my face.

When dusk darkened the white winter sky,
I'd slide down one last time through the hole
in the hedge and into my own backyard.
Mother would see me from the kitchen
and heat a mug of barley soup
to warm my icy hands.

That winter of my first blood
flowing, I carried my sled up from the cellar
when the first snow fell. As I waxed
metal runners with the white stub of a candle
Mother said I shouldn't ride anymore because
I was a woman now.

Climbing McKeever's that day
trailing the sled along
I looked up at the black-bordered windows
that seemed to be watching the children
slide down the hill.

The Waters of Childhood

When I think of the waters of childhood, the river comes first to my mind. The streets of Peekskill rose on the east bank of the Hudson River like trees with roots in the waters. My house was only two blocks from the river — two steep, long, winding blocks up a street everyone called Snake Hill. In a town built on hills this one was famous. Too treacherous for cars in the ice-covered snow, Snake Hill was claimed by children sledding all the way down to the railroad station by the river.

The regular click of the wheels on the tracks and deep-throated cries of train whistles carried me south along the river to New York City and north toward Poughkeepsie and the country beyond. I'd sit by the window and watch the flow of the river as the train swept me along. The water was smooth gray-green if I looked directly sideward out my window, yet shimmering blue if I looked out the window of the seat in front of me. We'd pass tugboats pushing their huge flat loads and sometimes on the western shore a silver engine pulled long white cars like the tail of a nearby comet.

Riding home from Grand Central Station, after the dark tunnel and the massive blocks of shadowy buildings, a narrow lane of water reflected whatever light was left in the sky. At first pinched by sheer palisades, the river quickly widened beneath ridges of gray boulders bulging through masses of trees, and then opened to the smooth layers of the Ramapo Mountains in shades of purple at nightfall.

The train moved swiftly past Dobbs Ferry and Tarrytown, past Sing Sing where my father served time before he met my mother. Always it paused at Harmon to change engines. Always the hiss of the steam and the small sudden jolt as the cars coupled. And then the slow, gentle rocking motion of those last few miles home.

When the trees were bare I could see the river from Mother's bedroom window. To the south lay the Ghost Fleet, large gray warships where tons of rotting wheat were stored. Northward on the opposite shore was Bear Mountain State Park. On clear winter nights I could see lights outlining the ski jump and flames from a skier's moving torch splitting the dark space between the lights.

Until my parents divorced when I was ten, we often went with my father to Bear Mountain Park for his summer weekend job as security guard. The State of New York saw fit to issue my father a gun, so I grew up with a gun in the top drawer of his dresser where he could grab it as easily as a pair of socks. To reach the Bear Mountain Bridge, he drove north over precarious mountain roads, often skirting ledges and stone walls. He made every trip a race — tires screeching, horn blasting — and we were his captives. Mother sat bolted next to him begging him to slow down. In the back my big brother sat up straight, knuckles white on the back of the seat in front of him, while I crouched down with my arms around my little brother. I'd peek out to see how far we had to go, and when I saw the river again I knew we were almost safe.

While Father roamed the park grounds in mirrored sunglasses and olive uniform, gun on hip, Mother took us to the playground, the zoo, the pool, and my favorite place, the lake. Hessian Lake was surrounded by tall pines and weeping willows whose slender branches bent down to the water. Near the rowboats a plaque explained that the lake was named after the German mercenary soldiers who were hired by the British during the Revolutionary War. The Colonists sank their boats as they rowed across the lake and their bodies were never found, giving rise to the legend that Hessian Lake is bottomless. It pleased me to think that here was a place where hired assassins could be made to vanish.

I'd walk around the lake and find a quiet place to sit and look at the reflections in the water. Around the rim the trees doubled in length in fluid shadows. The large, moving surface gently distorted the tone of the sky and patches of clouds. Even a breeze gave texture to the water and sun highlighted the shifting patterns.

If I drew close I would see a pale oval face, freckled as a fish. Small earrings where a gypsy had pierced, dark braided hair, teeth in braces that never did close the gap between them. Eyes the same changeable green as the lake, and like the lake, flecked with gold.

Beneath the surface of the water, another world: fleeting tadpoles and fuzzy moss on stones that looked in shifting, filtered light like tiny forests on small islands. I'd find a stone and toss it high, then watch it fall in the water, imagining it falling forever.

Wetlands

I
enter
and kneel
in the canoe
a dark fold
in light hands
— balance —
and push
the water back
to move forward
across the bay
shining and buoyant.
Here
no solid land intrudes
between puckered waves
and clouds shaped by wind.
Now and then wings
cross the sky
then suddenly
fall through the surface
of the sea
or a fish flings itself
up and out
and splashes down.
Here I am vast
vast as horizon
where reeds lash
the sky

Makani

You know about the heat
but do you know the wet song of the wind?
    When there is no rain, I listen
        for the wind that makes the sound of rain
           with blade and stalk and leaf.

I've been sleeping on the wind-
ward side for three dry weeks
    yet every morning the clacking of the palms
        wakes me with the patter of rain.

Noon sets my hair aflame
when I walk by the stream.
    Tall grass in the wind's breath
        whispers the rain.

Cane fields line a dusty road.
Green spears bend in the evening breeze
    then wave the wind across the field —
        swelling to a sea of rain.

Hawaiians name their children for the sea:
Nakai — of the sea, *Kainoa* — the sea is free.
    But if I bore a child here
        in the hot Hawaiian night,
           I'd name her *Makani* for the wind

Makani
    for the wind that sings the rain.

Bread

Everyone feeds the fat
white swan, long neck gliding
through the swirling
circus of small birds.
Ducks bob around it — iridescent
decoys in a carnival shoot
tipping heads under
for food. Gulls hover above
shrilling their hunger —
beak open, neck throbbing
and the wild insistent bead
of their eyes on my bread.

Harbor Island

None of the men spoke after Beth entered the car. No one touched her. No one even looked at her until the driver shut off the engine. Then he took his hands from the steering wheel, slowly turned his body toward the backseat, and stared at her.

Why had she taken the ride?

Her old bike had carried her to the last week of summer, but there wasn't time to fix a flat before work so Mrs. Hodge, her landlady, dropped her off at Hester's Diner. The locals Beth waited on there appeared friendly in spite of their New England formality. Though she knew she wasn't one of them, working as a waitress for the summer had meant she wasn't a tourist.

Feeling safe on Harbor Island, she decided to walk the two miles back to her cottage after work. Beth folded her red apron and stepped into the night. Nights were often chilly, but this one was warm. Tying the sleeves of her jacket around her waist, she breathed out cooking smells and breathed in the sea. Tips rested securely in the pocket of her cut-off jeans, leaving her free to swing her arms as she walked down the center of the road. She listened to the soft pad of her sneakers and the crickets.

The moon was full enough to light her way in the wide spaces between streetlamps and reflected brightly from her white blouse. It made her bare arms and legs look ivory. She played with the lengthening shadows and pretended a string stretched from the top of her head to the moon so she'd walk tall as the pine trees lining the road. The light frosted their needles, making Beth think she'd like to spend a winter on the island.

Placing a hand on each temple, she combed her long straight hair with her fingers, spread it into a fan — the air cooling her neck — and let it fall on her shoulders.

Yes, it had been a good summer. And now that it was almost over Beth could feel pleased that she had decided to live on her own for the first time. She'd had time to read and to sit by the shore. The motion of the waves reminded her of wheat fields in the wind, yet the ocean created a vast horizon that she had only dreamed about.

Is that the wind in the trees or the hum of a car? Beth tried to control an old fear. Her father used to follow her in his car after her parents' divorce, so she'd learned to look over her shoulder as she walked. Peeking through the classroom blinds, she'd check to see of his car was parked by the school yard, then sneak out the side door and race the two blocks home — chest aching, lungs burning. Alone in the house, she locked herself in and huddled beneath the kitchen table with her eyes closed.

Better to think about her twelfth summer, the summer her father finally left town. She had discovered a discarded bicycle in her neighbor's yard and painted it white. Her mom bought her a pair of green suede riding pants from the thrift shop. Beth rode that bike all summer as though it were the white stallion she'd always wanted.

Certain now that it was a car she was hearing, Beth moved toward the side of the road to get out of the way. She wished she were on her bike.

Headlights approached slowly, fixing her in their glare. A man's voice called out, "Need a ride?"

Squinting her eyes, she tried to see past the screen of lights, tried not to feel scared. Before she could answer, a head emerged from the driver's window and she recognized Brian. His family owned the general store and she had served them at Hester's.

Chiding herself for her fear, Beth took a step toward the car and said, "Brian, hi! My bike is broken so I'm walking back from work."

"Hop in. I'll give you a lift."

Beth had been enjoying the walk — until the car startled her. Maybe she'd been brave enough for one night, and she didn't want to seem unfriendly. Walking toward the car she said, "OK, thanks."

When the back door opened and a young man stepped out to hold the door, Beth moved away in surprise. Looking carefully into the car she saw there were two men in back and two in front.

As she hesitated, a voice spoke to her from the passenger side of the front seat. "Sorry about your bike. Anything I can do?"

It was Keith. He also ate at Hester's Diner, and he'd wave to her when they'd pass on their bikes.

"No thanks, Keith. I'll be able to buy another tire tomorrow if the patch won't hold. I just didn't want to chance it breaking again when I had to get to work."

Brian introduced the men in back as his friends. The one holding the door, a lanky fellow like her brother, wore thick glasses that looked too big for his face. She couldn't see the other one clearly. He tipped the visor of his cap and left it low on his forehead.

"I'm staying with Mrs. Hodge on Sweet Hollow Road," Beth said as she slid into the backseat. "Where are you guys going?"

The tall man squeezed in next to her and slammed the door. No one answered her. Brian put the car in gear and began driving very slowly down the road. Keith faced forward. Glancing to her left and right she saw that the men flanking her gazed straight ahead like mannequins. When she moved her feet she heard the dull clink of empty cans. The trousered legs on both sides still touched her though she pressed her thighs together. Wedged between their stiff forms, she focused on the road. *Oh no — how could I have been so stupid?*

They drove in silence past the windmill and the lightning-scarred tree that was her first landmark when she was learning her way around the island. As they drove past the turn for her street, Beth swallowed a sound that rose in her throat.

Keith looked out his side window for a moment. He switched on the radio, fiddled with the static, and snapped it off. The one with the cap began tapping an irregular beat on the metal window edge. The tall man moved in his seat and Beth felt the cloth of his slacks withdraw slightly from her skin.

Though the windows were open she didn't have enough air. *Breathe, breathe, breathe slowly.* The hair on her arms lifted in chilly patches and she felt suddenly naked in her shorts and sleeveless blouse.

Tires grated as they turned onto the dark gravel road. She wasn't sure if she was hearing the crash of the waves on the beach or her blood pounding in her ears. When the driver shut off the headlights Beth felt as though she were sitting in a dark theater. Then everything solid fell away. Like a plane's roar, a muffled din expanded painfully inside her head.

When the driver cut the engine, Beth thought the air was buzzing — like that day in the garden when she had pulled up the weeds — bees! She had tried to outrun them as they swarmed around her. Wildly she raked them from her hair and beat them from her body. As though on cue, they flew back into the hole in the earth. Still she'd heard a buzz, and looking down she saw a bee fly out of her blouse.

When Brian turned and faced her, his right hand gripped the back of the seat that separated them. Beth met his eyes but she could not read them. Locked in the shadow, she hoped he could see her, really see her. Terror steeled her.

Beth continued to hold his stare until Brian lifted his hand and then broke the silence with a hard slap against the top of the seat. Turning back to the wheel, he started the car with a lurch.

Beth felt dizzy. Her toes and fingers prickled as though they were thawing. Letting out her breath she slumped in her seat, almost relieved that a body was on each side of her.

They didn't touch her. They didn't say anything. None of them even looked at her as they dropped her off at the turn for Sweet Hollow Road.

Beth did not see them in the diner during her last week of work. For a long time she didn't speak about the ride. She never went back to the island. Still, her thoughts often returned to what they might have said to one another when they saw her that night on the road.

Stones

Here I walk on slabs of stone
not paths that lightly spring beneath my feet
and keep my step in rain.

No round stone
to hold in the palm of my hand
and skim across the surface of a pond.

Once I learned there are more
stars than grains of sand
on all the shores of earth.

Here it is not dark enough to see the stars.

Calling Up the Moon

Toss a stone in the water and circles spread across the sky.
Post a sign in the natural food store for women to meet
    on the shore when the moon is full.
One comes dancing over the sand,
    kicking her bare feet before her.
One brings a song, cradling a dulcimer.
One shares a large smooth melon, pale yellow orb
    passing hand to hand, sweet juice dripping,
        fingers and face washing in the sea,
            licking the salty sweetness on the skin.
One hands out bright scarves that fly after them as they run
    along the water's edge playing tag with the waves,
        a line of women curving like a snake on glassy sand.
One taps a small drum and one rattles a gourd
    and one shakes a tambourine trailing red ribbons
        high above her head.
And all of them bring their laughter
    and everyone brings her dreams.

On this first warm clear night
    the moon rises after dark has fallen.
Before it dims their light, stars appear like promises
    above the women forming mandalas on the shore.
Circles within circles spin with the rhythm of their feet
    and the rhythm of their song.
Sand paintings that move and scatter
    and remain in the mind.
One then two run into the sea. The others cheer
    then welcome the wet bodies into a circle
        of hands and towels that dry and warm.

Let's call up the moon!
The earth, the fire, the water, the sky
return   return   return   return

Silence. There, spreading on the horizon
    a disk of gold spilling along the surface of the sea.
Higher and higher it becomes a mirror of the circles
    they have been forming all night.
In the shadows of the moon's face, one woman sees
    the child she left sleeping in her mother's care,
One the embryonic curve of her desire,
One her husband's scowl as she walked out the door,
One sees her scars,
One the fragments of her self-destruction,
One the emblem of her ascending wholeness,
One the sea of her own tranquility,
And all of them see the singular beauty that monthly rounds
    into a circle of light.

Natural Bridge

for Louise

In Santa Cruz the ocean scallops the coast
into steep cliffs. Between the jagged half-
circles gouged from the land
sometimes the tide creates a natural bridge.

I walk along the cliffs with a woman
whose friendship spans a continent
for over twenty years, pacing our steps.
She says the distant blue mountains
are the clearest she's ever seen them.
I comment on the sturdy ground cover
blooming at our feet.

No Guarantees

I'm waiting for the muffler to be fixed —
waiting to see if this lifetime guarantee is a scam
or if they really will make good on the advertisement —
when a guy walks out of the shop and leans over
the big yellow car facing me, leans into the window
and kisses the girl in the driver's seat.
And he keeps kissing her with that open-mouth
head-rocking motion while the kid in the backseat —
maybe two years old — watches them, and then turns
to the toy in his hand, and when he looks back at them
they are still kissing: gray sweat pants pressing
hard against the car door,
blue tee shirt tight on his chest.
Metal is missing from the grill so it looks like
teeth knocked out,
the headlight is held in place with the same
black electrical tape that mends her sunglasses,
and the couple is still kissing —
her blondish curls and his slick dark hair moving
back and forth and around.
In her left hand she balances a white Styrofoam cup
on the door where the window goes down,
and her right hand holds the steering wheel —
cigarette smoldering between her fingers.
His bare arms are behind his back, so only their lips
and tongues and teeth are touching.
Then the kid picks up his bottle and sits there sucking,
watching them kiss.
      And I figure — whatthehell —
no guarantees, but it looks like love.

Lineaments of Desire

going down from the attic
you hold the ladder
as I descend
the afternoon light

we pause on the porch
to catch the sun as it falls
behind the horizon of houses
and I smile at the flashes
of copper in your beard

in the blinding brightness
you stand between me
and the sun setting
tendrils ablaze

a warm summer breeze
ruffles your hair
and the unbuttoned
loose fitting
striped cotton shirt
that covered your chest
all day in soft folds

as you lift your hand
to lean on the white
stucco wall of the house
the front of your shirt
like the flap of a tent
falls open

a slant ray of sun-
light shadows the hair
on the skin of your arm
and your chest
now bare   draws my glance

my eyes flicker down
to the curve of your breast
and the nipple at the center
of the cheek of your breast

looking away
then glancing again
my eyes alight
where my lips would linger

though I dare not
rest my head on the rise
of your chest
my eyes trace the naked
line of your flesh
to the nipple I would touch
with the tip of my tongue

Marvelous Beast

suspended from
      your animal form
           arms and legs circling
      bodies touching
           then glancing away

the tease of your nearness
      and parting excites me
           and now I am striding
      at ease with your bigness
my pleasure spreading
           in widening spheres

and now we are moving
      faster and faster
           though still unhurried
      knowing this lasts
knowing how far
           we can ride

and now I am
      urging you enter
           the quickening center
      everything in me
           shaped to an O

After the Flood

The day we left the mountain
        mist rose from drenched hay
                water beads sparkled in cornfields.

Floods broke bridges
        so we had to poke till we found
                dry ground to cross.

All day the sun smoldered in the gray sky.

At evening it turned a great luminous peach
        then a shadowy strand of damp hair
                I brushed from your forehead.

Lucid Dream: Desert

Hot and dry and stark...I see myself in a busy gathering on the bleached sand...building small shelters of pole and cloth...*Is this a bazaar?* the dreamer wonders while the woman in the dream knows where she is, goes about her task

I see a man setting up his tent near mine...he wears a long white robe like my own...his face lined with years of the sun, peering into the night...we help each other with familiar ease...bind wind-flapping blankets of faded beige to poles with rope

Are we in a gypsy camp?...we are Bedouins, the dreamer decides, and then I become the woman living the dream

Glaring sunlight dims to soft pinks and violets of desert dusk ...the rest of the tribe vanishes...only our two simple tents stand in the silent expanse

I lie on my back under the canopy on a thin mattress... relaxed and aware...you walk toward me...stretch out full length on top of me...your heavy body covers me completely, chest and thighs...I am completely comfortable with your weight...as though the sky has come down onto me

Dark night deepens vivid threads of blue and red in faded cloth...then our tents disappear...I rest between earth and cloudless starless moonless sky

Your lips moisten my lips...I open my mouth...your tongue slowly circles between my lips and teeth...circles the cave of my mouth...ridges on the roof like windswept sand...soft flesh inside my cheeks

The warmth of your kiss spreads down my body...my throat becomes a pueblo with terraces and windows and ladders... my chest a landscape of cliff dwellings...down down through layers of buried cities...outlines of foundations...ancestral mounds

Beyond the layers of civilization...beyond the layers of stone ...parting the dense broken layers of stone...you above me thick as thunder...descending into a sea of fire

You Bring Me Back

You bring me back
to my early pleasure.
Deep in the night
I climb the high
chair of your lap
and rest in sure
familiar dreams.

When I turn, you turn
and I become host
to your sleeping
body, your naked body.
Kneading the flesh
aligning the bones
till morning arouses
a shape, a smell
and we turn to each other
in familiar pleasure.

Seeds

We finally got around to planting sunflowers.
Along the back fence most formed puny stalks,
ankle high, with shells stuck on top like paper hats.
Three grew knee high
then fell on their faces in comical flops.

Along the side fence one giant golden head
nodded over weathered wood all of August.
We meant to take a picture, but never did.
This fall John built a darkroom in the basement.
Next year we'll be sure to take pictures.

We had enough tomatoes to feed the neighborhood —
gazpacho and sauce and salads all summer, then
the last green ones rescued before the frost.
I soaked basil and cucumbers in vinegar,
froze parsley and dill for winter soup.

Blue morning glories flourished, but I had to catch them
before they puckered against the sun.
Virginia gave me seeds from her night-
blooming moonflowers
so something was always opening.

I saved the seeds,
labeled blue envelopes,
and stored them in a shoe box in the darkroom.

The Wonders of Infinite Smallness

Halfway around the world you
send news of our son's thoughts
on infinite smallness —
how all things can be
made smaller, how the tiniest
particle can be reduced to the point
where we cannot see it, how
the universe could have exploded from a speck
and perhaps now the whole
world containing all that
exists could be compressed to the size
of a golf ball,
and would it all be miniature
or scrunched like scrapped cars.

Halfway around the world I
miss you both, miss being home.
On a journey for a month to a distant country
retreat, I feel close when I read your words.
And the photograph you sent of our son
holding his newborn cousin,
cradling the small body in his now big hands,
I placed against the mirror of the night-
stand at the foot of my bed.
His eyes
look back at me,
head tilting slightly, strands of hair
falling on his forehead,
lips curved in a wonderful smile.

My host had placed a wooden Buddha (serene
hands cupped in lap) next to the mirror,
and now this picture balances the statue.
Reduced from the original, composed of charm
particles of black and white and silver grays,
his picture grounds me. When I call home
he says, "Are you safe?" and wonders
how our voices fly across the sea.
I tell him about the calf mooing for its mother
in the neighboring meadow
while she is down the road bellowing back.
And as we speak I feel you both
could be in this room, so small
the distance.

In the Doorway

Standing in the doorway, afraid
of breaking his sleep,
I listen to my son's labored breath.

The first time I cradled him in my arms
I watched the sun rise along the spine
of the tall pine across the way.

And the first time he was sick
I ran the shower for steam
and held his head up all night.

Now he thinks he's too old
to be told when
to go to bed, when to wear a hat.

Back in my bed I try not to think
of the lifeless child my friend found
in the crib.   He saw his son
stand alone just once —
one triumph over gravity.

Toward morning
I listen at my son's door again
and he is snoring like an old man.

For My Son Who Wants To Be Rich

Rich is

toilet paper in the linen closet
when you need it

milk money in the blue cup by the phone

a closet   a phone   a blue cup.

Bequest

after the confusion of being
gripped by the throat on the school bus
Jew words spit in his face
>*say you're a Jew — say it—*
>*say Hitler was right!*

after the shame of looking away
when teammates mocked kids in beanies
at play across the field
and learning to laugh at jokes
he didn't get
>and didn't want to

he found himself fleeing his nightmare
where boots kicked down doors
women cried aloud
and the graybeard pointed at his back
>running from the house of horror

cursing me for cursing him
>with the burden of his story

after this dream he came to be
friendly with a neighbor
and walked with him three times to *shul*
and home to bless the bread
>and talk around the Shabbos candles

now tonight he invites me to temple
where we sit in the solitude of light
deepening gold to red as one by one
just enough gather to sing aloud
and he is proud of being
>the necessary one

perhaps another day may find a boy
running to his door at evening
calling him to stand with nine
who want to say a Kaddish
      though he may not return till then

he says he's gonna make a million
      and I wish him luck
tonight it is good to know
      my son made a minyan

Palm Reading

Gypsies traced a troubled childhood
and early independence
in the creases of my palm. My life
would be eventful and long —
one said difficult but worthwhile.

I was to have two children
(one died inside me,
the other stands beside me)
and three great loves.

They always saw the same three
great loves. At first I thought
three was many, but now
I wonder: is three enough
for a life so eventful and long?

And maybe love means something other
than a man's voice calling up my dreams.
Maybe it means passion that opens the sky
and shows me how stars are formed

Summer Storms

This storm reminds me of another. Years ago
I took shelter at my brother's
after I'd lost the child.
                              Thunder woke us
all except my niece who'd dragged her sleeping
bag out to the porch and made a den
where she could see the stars. Instead
jagged streaks lit voluminous clouds.
My brother scooped her up and held her
against his chest while she slept
through the booming storm, her face
nuzzled in his neck. Her damp hair
matted on his cheek was dark
as the rabbit she'd let me stroke that day.
Proud of its beauty and clearly in love
she freed the gentle feral creature
from its cage. Then from the safety
of her embrace offered it for my touch.

Now this storm long beyond that time
when tenderness was balanced in their arms
brings me back to feral creatures
and my brother's sudden show of love
electrified in flashes.

Touched by Zero

No matter how many
march along the rim of the hill
zero follows like a hungry shadow

Patient steadfast absolute
it collects the bill
charged at birth

One brother then two
One two three fathers
A child in my small round womb

Any one touched by zero
equals zero
in time

Weight

After walking with Helen through green
meadows, earth yielding to our step,
we part as she turns toward her home
and I toward mine.

Inside the old house I see trees
through every window's wavy glass
and think how lovely
to stay here forever watching the seasons
flower and flame.

Moving through comfortable rooms
I meet a man composed
of men I've known, and he asks,
"Do you feel the weight of the world
will be less when you leave?"

as though he knows my body
has been drifting away —
I've been squinting at numbers and wincing
when I touch the surgeon's cut.

Again I find myself walking toward home
carrying my nearly-grown son
in my arms, but he is a miniature
of himself
              and he is light
lighter than when he was born.

He grows to full size
when I place him in the center
of the bed. I tuck the quilt around him
and watch his breath
rise and fall.

Threshold

Well I remember
>> her holding me, rocking me
> awash in her soft silent
>> darkness and sound

Before I was born
> I breathed in her water
salt on my skin
> my body becoming

A child I felt
> breathed in me too
well I remember
> crying out *Mama*

At the last threshold
> I will step from the shore
to that same reservoir
> home of all waters

from

When the Light Falls Short of the Dream

(1998)

Don't Slip Away

In the still green September
I held on to summer
by the hem of her gown,
lingering like a child
in the last light of play,
before flannel sheets
and the snap of the storms.

In the still green September
I dropped off my mother
and she waved me on.
Don't slip away,
I heard myself say,
don't skip away
don't slip away

Fall Back

You can squander the hour you've saved
on sleep. You can let it slip till morning
then casually flick back the clock.

But if you wait for an hour you want
to linger, and savor the time
you've reclaimed from spring

you'll have that hour
to fall back on
when the light falls short of the dream.

Late at Night

The muffled cadence of your voice
as you talk on the phone
filters down from the attic
through my bedroom ceiling.
Not words, but sometimes cooing
and sometimes an earnest crescendo
resonates in the long tunnel
night stretches from sundown to dawn.
No tires whine in the street.
No engine drones in the sky.

Late at night the house is silent
except for your father's soft
breathing in and out beside me
and the comforting sound of you
still perched beneath the eaves.

My Son's Shadow

My son's shadow stretches out
from where he stands praying
at the edge of the pool of light
cast by the evening lamp.
Swaying gently, his shadow leans
toward the compact book he holds
firmly in his hands.

He does not see me where I sit
rocking on the porch
to the rhythm of his voice
that clarifies the deepening dark.
It is enough that I see his shadow stretch
across the floor and up the wall
to the ceiling and beyond

The Nape of His Neck

Shaving his neck I am girl again
sister to the smell of my brother's skin
buffed and creamed to a clean sweetness —
my first whiff of male.

Later the friendly ritual of grooming
husband and wife in a prelude to pleasure,
shaver in one hand, the other hand free
to stroke the sleek trails.

Now my son who is nearly a man
offers the nape of his neck for my care
and I surrender once more to the throb
that swells in my throat.

Turning Fifty

How your deaths press me.
Brothers who died young
in your sleep. Or worse —
awake in the night
still struggling with hurt
unhealed from our first
dangerous family.

When the blanket of death
smothered you, in bed
with a woman
not your wife —
and you, wrestling all night
with your unsigned will —
what did you grasp?

Now I'm the oldest.
I think of you
as boys: big brothers
who smelled of shaving.
One a bully
the other a tease.
I never knew you as men.

Now, at fifty,
I think of you often.
Not only how you died
but how we lived
so far apart.
Even as children.
Even at fifty.

Apples

Green & gnarled as a fist
they make the house shudder
when they thud to the earth.

Fall knocks.

Wild November Leaves

Yellow hankies
in women's outstretched hands
waving their men to war.

Brave. Furious. Lost.

The Burning

Franticly waving
the slight young man whips his shirt
wildly above his dark body.

Open-mouthed drivers
slow to a crawl as they pass
the fiery car.

Stretched out for miles
at the brink of overheating
travelers curse their luck.

Screaming red lights
clear a jagged path through clots of traffic
as they move toward the flames.

Looking for God on the other side
of the Whitestone Bridge.

The List of Names:
Jean (1925-1995)

Everything tasted of ash.
I never looked up at the sky
the whole time I was in Auschwitz.

When my period stopped
I was so afraid
I'd never have children.

Mengele saw me naked
more than my husband
in all the years we've been married.

Of my family only I survived
to wear the coat
lined with names.

After the war we wandered
scavenging for food
and places to sleep.

No one wanted us.
Now the children don't want to hear.

The Other Dream

Inside the barren room
people we know are reading your words
and making speeches in your honor.
When I try to enter
the doorkeeper tells me my name
is not on the list,
and when I look for you in the room
you are not there.

So I look for you in another dream
where you are in the living
room of your home, host
to a circle of friends.

Last Morning in Jerusalem

The hotel faces the Old City
where my son feels at home
among the stones and trees.
Which ones did my pennies plant
from the blue tin cans of youth,
each one placed by other hands?

Light rain burnishes
the pink and golden stones,
freshens the parched earth.

Turning from the window, I pack
the Kiddush cup, replicas of Miriam and Moses,
the moss green stones from Eilat —

richer and poorer for leaving.
Jerusalem, I give you my son.

You Call from a Phone Booth

You call from a phone booth in Jerusalem
and say there's a blackout. (I look at the dark
and picture bombs streaming from the sky
like last week in the north
where rockets from Lebanon
flattened homes to foundations of stone.)
You say it's just a power failure.

Earth, fire, ocean, sky,
please don't let him die.

When I wake up later that night
the earth has turned your way
and moonlight from a bright full moon
streams through my bedroom window.
Looking east I can see you
standing on the gold stones of Jerusalem
bathed in golden light.

The Comfort of Time Zones

Just as I get into bed at midnight
you call and say that it's dawn.
After we talk I am able to sleep
knowing you're safe in tomorrow.

Seasons

1
back door geraniums
break the winter grip of spring
with bold red fists

2
August sunset
flames the rippling bay
liquid pinks and gold

3
wind-riffled hemlocks
graceful peacock feathers
green in autumn's fan

4
skin pressed warm on skin
then fetch the morning paper
barefoot in snow

The Guest

I open the door and white
covers my steps.
An overnight guest
has rolled out his blanket
on my living room floor
built the fire
and now he is cooking
a meal for us.

What do I do?
I let him
keep his boots by my door.

The Let-Down Response

That winter on the farm I watched
the farmer grip one swollen teat
in each of his large bony hands,
fingers wrapped firmly on the downstroke,
gently on the up, till
the cow let go of her milk
and filled the metal pail
with the sweet rhythmic sound of release.

Ginger

you lay me on the table
and make my bones click

I close my eyes and rise
to a cool dim place

your fingers touch my temples
and leave a pungent memory

of the ginger on your skin
from handing your daughter a sweet

her laughter in the next room
tinting the air opal and jade

and ginger ginger ginger

We Grew Up

We grew up so close
your window was the light I looked for
through the maze of branches
in nights veiled with doubt.
I stood beneath that window
as you practiced your horn,
notes floating around me
like petals in spring.
When you left the valley
I missed the timbre of your voice.
Tonight the phone was your window,
the light was still on,
and I gave a holler.

The Hunter

The deer head mounted on the wall caught me
in the brown glass of his eye and held my gaze
on delicate features of his face, the sweep
of neck, antlers like a crown of flames —

regal woodland creature, graceful totem,
humble welcome to our country cabin.

They say the man who shot that deer died killing
deer. Ten years ago at seventy-five
he raised his bow, aimed, let loose an arrow
then slipped on ice and cracked his naked head.

That's the story townsfolk tell. But neighbors
living up the hill who watch this house
for signs of life say Jake died a different
way, not the rugged frontier way.

These neighbors are the ones who found the wife
slumped over solitaire at the kitchen table
five years later. I like to think they know
what happened to the man who killed this deer.

Yes, it was in winter, icy too,
and Jake was known to hunt with bow and arrow,
but this is how he died: he tripped and fell
and whacked his head while lugging out the trash.

Watching Him Handle Stones

Shirtless on the first day of summer
he bends and grips the large flat stone.
Muscles tense, he lifts it
and turns it over in his hands
to fit the contours of the garden wall
then slips it into place.

When a sudden shower drives us in
steam rises from the warm earth
and I feel solid and light in his hands
as he fits the bare contours
of his body to mine.

If I Do Nothing

If I do nothing
blades of grass will pierce the earth,
wind will tousle leaves
and make the branches bow.

If I do nothing
light will shift throughout the day
brightening colors
then bathing them in shade.

Dragonflies will flit
from stream to blossom to stone,
spiders spin silk
and birds let fly their song.

If I do nothing
but witness the deep-throated
beauty of iris
God will still tend the earth.

The Formation of Stars

I dream we are traveling through desert
on a moving carpet of sand
when I turn to you and ask
how did we fall in love?
and you say it had something to do
with the formation of stars

stars? I say looking up at the vast
evening sky as it darkens from azure to ink,
and there where the sky touches sand
piercing a wide band of cobalt —
a singular radiance

that can't be a star, I say,
too big, too bright, and besides
with more stars than grains of sand
there would be more

then you take my hand
and we turn toward the light

NEW POEMS

Make Your Way Across This Bridge

Mysteries

Nothing Broke

All the girls slept together
in the lace bedrooms of childhood
and later when we nodded off
on the playroom couch —
head resting on a shoulder,
face nuzzling into the curve
of neck, sweet-smelling hair
splayed across the pillow we shared.

Was there a nest beneath the eave
that brought the bird to flutter
at the glass? Nothing broke
the rhythmic rising of our breasts
the harmony of breath
the tangling of our dreams.

Fools Rush In

A door cracks open
in the side of a dream —
Clinton's face appears
with his hello darlin' eyes

I slide down his smile
into the darkened theater
where love-me-tender Elvis sings
with one dark eyebrow raised

When he looks at me and bites
his bottom lip between his teeth
I am fire in the face and
wet below

That's why the girls who felt the throb
as we sat alone in the dark,
head tipped back, mouth open,
understood when Monica knelt

Women Will Fall Open

Women will fall open before him
like unabridged dictionaries
craving the comfort
of a flat spine.

When he spans them
will his fingers tease the meanings
from the lines of blood and bone?

Mysteries

When he sleeps with a woman
   a mystery unfolds.

Will he feel a new tenderness
   temper his hardness when he wakes?

He sleeps with a woman
   who bleeds a mystery.

What promise will she hold?
   What promise will he keep?

The First Time

The first time he came inside me
the finger of God poked a hole
right through the rubber sheath.
When he pulled out
we couldn't find it
on his flesh or in the bed
so I had to fish with my finger
till I caught the ring.

Calling Out Your Name

forty years after I pressed
a pillow between my thighs
calling out your name
you slip inside my dream
for a sure coupling

a hint of beard
brushes my cheek, my neck,
breath fills my ear
and a slow blush
spreads down my throat

I wake up laughing
at a first taste of passion
so strong
that forty years later
it spices my dream

Turnings

Of all the sweet turnings
offered by nature and night to tired bodies
this one I savor — turning toward you
    and finding you warm
        rising with breath

Bound on that borderless plane
our bodies flow north to the stream
that pulses and churns by our window —
    we drift together
        raft on the current of night

Bruised Sky

My Father's Coins

jangled in his pockets
as he walked down the stairs.

I would wait at the bottom
and beg him

to dig down in his pocket
and find some change.

I'm sure there were times
he put a penny in my palm

or why would I remember
begging?

Bruised Sky

Bruised sky overhead —
winter afternoon bleeds
into winter night

Silent Night

Little girl scared
breathing in the dark
sharp smells of the women's ward.
To comfort herself in the strange silence
she hums a familiar song.

The slow descending melody
vibrating in her chest
lengthens her breath and quiets the worried
words of her mother and her doctor
and her father's blows.

The girl begins to sing the soothing
words, lingering on *tender* and *mild*.
In the metal bed at the end of the ward
her small voice
sweetens the silence

until a starched white cap in the doorway
shouts, "Who's that singing? Quiet!"
The child hides her head
beneath the thin covers, barely
breathing through the cords of her throat.

Does she imagine the other women joining
in chorus? Young wives, overwhelmed,
recovering from surgery,
delicate old ladies praying
for heavenly peace.

Someone We Love

Another one wants to die.
How little I can do to stop the downward slide.
Your only connection's with dogs? Then tether yourself
to them. Volunteer at the shelter.
Get out of the cell of yourself.
I'm full of suggestions, but
when I hang up the phone and rush to work
the faces in the hallway mirror my fear —
we who are trying to keep someone we love alive.

Eyes darting or shut tight, we huddle
in a corner cradling a phone clamped to the ear.
Everywhere I look I see this face,
like when I was pregnant and the whole world was
pregnant. Bellies bulged wherever I looked.
Selective perception, I know —
when you buy a car or hear a new word
suddenly you notice that new thing everywhere.

But that's it, I implore the sad ones,
the damaged, angry, frightened, downed out,
disappointed, hopeless ones —
the world is full of *everything
all the time*. The air is rich with frequencies
and our mind a receiver that can
pick up different signals if we turn the dial.
Ariel heard song on the enchanted isle and
you can too.

And after the pleas, the rage — How dare you
toss away your gift, your spark in the eternal light.
Open your eyes!
Wake up to your life!
Grab hold, dear one, tether yourself to life.

Some Prayers Are Answered

some trip on the tongue
some stick in the throat
some prayers are swallowed

some born in the soul
make the heart swell
some roar from the gut

some prayers escape in a sigh
for the child who turns
toward the dark

some hover in the shallow breath
we hardly dare to breathe
for the one in danger

alone on the road
in his room
in his head

some endure
some are lost
some find their way home

The Price

for Mary and Philip

The last of seven cygnets — tawny thing
that we'd seen grow from wingless featherball
to dusky swan — preens his coat
on the bank of the pond where his parents molt.
Settled in the scattered white, he lifts a wing
revealing his first white feathers.

One by one the other cygnets disappeared,
just like the goslings before them, all the broods
of three or four that paraded after the geese.
Once I saw a hawk swoop down and pin a goose
by its neck with one claw, then pierce
a gosling with the other and carry it off —

When the cygnets disappeared I pictured each one
caught up in the talons of a hawk's descent,
but maybe a muskrat pulled one under water
or a fox crept along the bank.

As the swans glide across the pond
with their only child, the phantoms of the other
six push the sole survivor closer to the mother
while father follows. When the little one feeds,
snaking his neck into the water and tipping
his tail toward the sky, the parents stay near —
head turning on long neck
like a radar tower scanning for danger.

Snapping turtles practice parenting
a different way. One, big as a pizza,
crawled up from the pond at dawn, dug a hole
in the soft soil of the garden with her hind legs,
deposited half a dozen eggs, covered them with earth,
and crawled back to the pond.
The fate of turtle eggs is precarious
but this mother didn't stay. By morning
the hole was empty — probably plundered
by the racoon that forages in my garbage.

My neighbor who shares the pond is waiting
to bring her adopted daughter home
from the other side of the world. She's painted
gossamer fairies in her room and built a fence
and planted a garden and given her a name.
And I think of the voyage they will have
together, and the price of vigilance
my friend will have to pay for parenthood.

Because

Because a puppy is *now!* while the news
is grief for yesterday and fear
for tomorrow, we drive to the animal shelter
the Sunday after the towers collapse.
The shelter is packed with children
eager to make a dog wag its tail
or be licked by a cat's sandpaper tongue.
Parents who had said no or when you're older
are eager to give their kids something
to watch besides the rising toll.

I'd heard the news in the car as I drove home
from my second radiation treatment
and it seemed unreal at first, unreal
as the news in August when a smiley-face
computer voice announced, "You've got cancer!"
— unreal until the surgeon cut
the nodule from my breast and I could feel
the tender reality. It's small, he said,
a pea or a pearl, or a nuclear reactor I thought
and where else are they lurking, these ticking bombs?

September explosions and the thousands dead
make the threat inside my body seem smaller,
so we stop in front of a sleepy chocolate pointer
with white patches on her face and chest
and the tip of her tail. Careful for the stitches
in her belly, we place her on the table where she
shakes off sleep and invites us to fall in love.
Before we walk out with her in my arms, a sign
warns, "Are you ready for a fifteen-year commitment?"
and I say sure, I'll take it — give me fifteen years.

The Endless Horizon

Intimacies

Light in the heavy hospital bed, so light
she seems to float beneath thin blankets —
frail reflection on pale walls.

I moisten her lips,
stroke her cheeks,
brush the new hair back from her forehead.

She asks for a small mirror. I place
the pewter handle of my mother's oval mirror
in her hand.

She tells me she hopes her son remembers her laughing,
that her daughter had come 'round,
how pleased she is a grandchild inherited her spirit.

We do not speak — as we often did —
of the husband she had to care for
through the lonely years

but of the lover who turned from her
now when she needs him.
I do not ask his name.

Just before dying she laughs and says
I'm so delicious she'd like to lick me
down the entire length of my body.

A Sleeping Child

Never wake a sleeping child —
    that's what my mother told me.

A sleeping child is a sacred child —
    that's what my mother told me.

Now as I watch my child sleep
    I feel her arms enfold me.

Afterimage

I watch him walk the long block to the *shul*
through sunny patches between the row of trees.
When he turns right his white jacket disappears —
his afterimage lingers

Usually he looks back and waves as he rounds the corner.
Today the shadows of autumn leaves
wave on sidewalk squares
in changing patterns of light and shade

Moving Day

Solomon chose an understanding heart.
God made him wise as well.
I fear I have too little wisdom,
too much understanding.

Your guidance counselor chided me for being *too*
understanding. That became a joke between us
when you'd get your way and when I did for you
what you should have done.

How hard to strike a balance. Letting go,
holding on, holding up, holding back.
I remember chaffing at my mother's fearful
cautions, tried not to pass them on to you.

When you were two I went with her to Israel.
At the Dead Sea the bus ran late, no time
for a bathing suit. I hiked my long skirt up my thighs —
started wading in —

"Patti, you'll get your skirt wet!" Mother shouted
from the bus. We laughed about that scene for years,
then I had a chance to play it back: Fifteen,
on your own in Jerusalem, you called from a bus station

when a girl invited you down to the seaside town of Eilat.
From the other side of the world I pushed away
the image of a bus strewn across the road
and said, "Go get your pants wet."

Moses and Jesus, standing on the shore,
come to mind today. Turning to Moses,
Jesus asks how to do it, and Moses tells him,
"Walk on the rocks."

My rabbi taught me God's a metaphor
for God, said the Red Sea was a reed sea
and Moses knew the tides, making the passage
even more wonderful.

Find the solid places, slippery though they be —
life is washed with blood and tears.
Learn the tides.
Get your pants wet.

The Endless Horizon

I slide through the wave —
   O the water is jade
      the water is jade!

Pearls of air
   bubble around me
      dissolving the body that bound me

Buoyant and free
   borne on the sea
      the endless horizon of God

Long Beach

Sunset at our backs —
our bodies make long shadows
stretch across the sand

Along the boardwalk
honeycomb windows reflect
the sun descending

Before us the gulls
scatter in graceful patterns
like unfolding fans

For twenty-five years
we've walked by the sea on this
narrow strip of land

Now beneath a sky
tender with the blush of pink
you reach for my hand

Notes to the New Owners

This house is old. It is not plumb.
Steam hisses softly from the radiators
like a contented dragon.
When you toss your son over your shoulder
and carry him smiling up the stairs to bed
the steps will creak beneath your feet.

But I will warrant you this: The house is sound
as a Greek ship. That's what the man who stomped
around these floors said as he thumped the walls and lifted
his eyes to the high ceilings: "They just don't build them
this way any more."

From your bedroom window you can watch the moon fly
across the black sky. Summer draws a maple curtain
till fall when you can see stars tangle in the limbs.
Open the window and listen for birds, crickets.
The waves that slap the shore will rock you all to sleep.

I grew up in a dark and dangerous house.
Here the morning sun throws rainbows on the kitchen walls;
afternoons the southern rooms are bathed in light.
Plant your shade lovers in the front — impatiens, fuchsia.
The back garden will bloom in perennial surprise.

In this home I've spent my happiest years.
Here our son took his first step the day we moved in
and grew to be a good man.
Here my mother grew to a glad old age.
Here we slept in one another's arms.

We hand you the keys with our blessing:
May yours be a joyful home, a loving home, a sanctuary.

Home

Two months after we sell the Beech Street house
I drive past. A glance reveals
windows light the dusk,
their books fill the bookcase,
flower pots bloom on the bluestone steps.

I pull over across the street. Yes,
they've made it their own.
Peace envelops the house as evening falls.
And then this gift: A big man with a beard
comes around the corner carrying his son.
In tee shirt and shorts they'd been to the beach
to catch the setting sun. The boy reaches
his arms around his father's neck
as they bounce along the sidewalk to their home.

Cabin Nights

Drawn to the silk of your skin
    my body follows your hollows and hills
        warm in the early chill

All the night creatures
    bound in the breathing air
        end their song in country silence

Through the lingering stillness
    I catch the rush of the swollen stream —
        water smoothing stones

Night's Eye

Outside my window birds call.
Go to your day, I tell them.
Fling yourself dizzy.
Sweep the empty sky.
I want to stay in night's eye.

Smallwood

When we arrive
the horseshoe creek that bends
around our cabin in the woods
is laced with ice, closing in
on the dark water pulsing
through the center of the bed.

We sleep beneath a sky of stars.
When we wake a fine snow
is sifting from the metal sky.

Gray slate courtyard,
brown bark,
the roof of the red cabin
and all the greens that dare
to stay alive in winter — white.

The flower beds you worked
so hard to grow and covered
in fall with stubbly hay,
smoothed beneath a sheet of snow.
Beyond the garden the trees
reveal their elegant scaffold.

Within this still, small world
we have weathered another year
with love and luck and will.

Greedy

We leave this life with what is
in the pockets of the heart.
Untie the laces, undo the button,
this one is dead.

Papa would say that life is
ky und shpy, chew and spit,
then he'd close his eyes
and turn his face toward the sun.

We spend a lifetime learning what dogs know.
The map of warm light on the floor
as it moves through the day, the sound
of a key unlocking the door,
taste of fingertips and cheek,
the pleasure of caress.

The life I chose is rich
in harmonies and contradictions.
The life life chose for me has fistfuls
of feeling both joy and surrender,
explosive surprise and islands of peace.

When people ask if I'm afraid of death
I say death is nothing. How can I be
afraid of nothing? I'm afraid of losing life.
Life is something and I am greedy,
greedy for the something of life.
Not the trinkets, but what we carry
in the pockets of our heart.

Index of Titles

A Brief Walk   87
After He Left My Bed   71
Afterimage   194
After the Flood   130
Apples   155
Ask the Dreamer Where Night Begins   60
A Sleeping Child   193
August   34
Because   190
Bequest   139
Beware of Lovers   74
Birds and Leaves   42
Blind Trust   96
Braiding   28
Bread   117
Bruised Sky   184
Cabin Nights   201
Calling Out Your Name   180
Calling Up the Moon   123
Cat in a Dream Shop   43
Clenched   64
Cosmic Dancer   24
Crazed Mirrors   11
Dark Pages   31
Desire Followed Me Home   47
Don't Slip Away   149
Down My Mother's Hall   39
Driving Across the Texas Night   9
Embarrassed by Dreams   48
Eros and Civilization   3
Fall Back   150
Family Circle   23
Father's Day   22
First Love   27

Fools Rush In 176
For My Son Who Wants To Be Rich 138
Found Money 109
Garden 79
Gifts 107
Ginger 166
Go Gently Toward Death 57
Greedy 204
Harbor Island 118
Helen's Beauty 13
Home 200
How Odd This Ritual of Harmony 15
I Am Your Witness 59
I Can't Believe the Moon 93
If I Do Nothing 170
I have touched 91
In the Doorway 137
Intimacies 192
Invitation 65
It Flies 70
I woke up 50
Last Morning in Jerusalem 160
Late at Night 151
Laughing Thoroughbreds 4
Legacy for Louise 12
Lineaments of Desire 127
Living with a Poet 81
Long Beach 198
Long Beach, Long Island 36
Looking at the Fence 89
Love Allows 16
Love Finds a Place 5
Lucid Dream: Desert 131
Makani 116
Marvelous Beast 129
McKeever's Hill 110
Men Against the Sky 54
Missiles Cruise Toward Cuba 62

Morning Warmth   21
Moving Day   195
Museum   51
My Father's Coins   183
My Mother's Song   40
My Son's Shadow   152
Mysteries   178
Natural Bridge   125
Newborn   18
Night's Eye   202
No   90
No Guarantees   126
Notes to the New Owners   199
Nothing Broke   175
Old Habits Die Hard: Milk   95
Palm Reading   141
Pause   75
Piercing the Night   52
Possibilities of Pink   45
Post Humus   80
Raining Leaves   58
Rosa Parks   35
Seasons   163
Secret Passages   41
Seeds   134
Sewing the Bullet Holes   55
Silent Night   185
Silver Dollars   108
slender reed   10
Smallwood   203
Snowbound   49
Someone We Love   186
Some Prayers Are Answered   187
Still at Night   73
Still Life   33
Stones   122
Stopped at a Light   32
Streetlight   100

Subway   105
Summer Storms   142
Summoned from Sleep   20
Sweet Burden   26
Talisman   30
That One Tree   53
The Big Woman   44
The Book of Clouds   103
The Burning   157
The Comfort of Time Zones   162
The Endless Horizon   197
The First Time   179
The Formation of Stars   171
The Guest   164
The Hunter   168
The Last Tear   69
The Lesson   61
The Let-Down Response   165
The Line   19
The List of Names: Jean (1925-1995)   158
The Nape of His Neck   153
The Other Dream   159
The Price   188
The River   85
The Small Bed   104
The Turnkey   8
The Waters of Childhood   113
The Window   63
The Wonders of Infinite Smallness   135
The Words   67
This Year   88
Those Gypsy Eyes   29
Threshold   145
Till Death Do Them Part   14
Tonight   98
Torn Pictures   17
Touched by Zero   143
Tropism   6

Tuesday 76
Turning Fifty 154
Turnings 181
Upon the Occasion of Your First Birthday 25
Vanishing Point 66
Watching Him Handle Stones 169
We Grew Up 167
Weight 144
Western Window 99
Wetlands 115
We Touch by Accident 7
White Cranes 77
White Space 97
Wild November Leaves 156
Wild Promises 78
Women Will Fall Open 177
You Bring Me Back 133
You Call from a Phone Booth 161
You Like a Man 46

Index of First Lines

A door cracks open   176
After he left my bed   71
after the confusion of being   139
After walking with Helen through green   144
All month long the sky blistered   34
All the bright day I rode my bike along the river   85
All the girls slept together   175
Almost every day I find   109
And at the end   the words   67
Another one wants to die   186
a small body of land   62
Awakening this morning   21
back door geraniums   163
Because a puppy is *now!* while the news   190
Behind our house on Simpson Place   110
Between the legs of our property   41
Born in 1945   59
Born of feathered violence   13
Bruised sky overhead —   184
Cardinals light   42
Carrying my child to bed tonight   26
crazed mirrors   11
Curse you father   31
Darkness down my mother's hall beckons   39
Desire followed me home —   47
Drawn to the silk of your skin   201
Embarrassed by dreams   48
Everyone feeds the fat   117
Everything tasted of ash.   158
forty years after I pressed   180
Franticly waving   157
From my porch   70
From my porch I see men walk against the sky   54
going down from the attic   127
Green & gnarled as a fist   155
Gypsies traced a troubled childhood   141

213

Halfway around the world you   135
He sees the long legs and the trim   105
Here I walk on slabs of stone   122
He shook the keys at me   8
He was going to leave, but fearing it   14
Hot and dry and stark   131
how greenly the tree   27
how many times   4
How your deaths press me.   154
I   115
I awaken   10
I can't believe the moon   93
I conjured up your image   98
I'd forgotten the streetlight, forgotten   100
I dream we are traveling through desert   171
I drove my son to school so he could stay warm   76
If I do nothing   170
If this city were an island   36
I have not seen him since I was ten   17
I help him match his morning tie   64
I'm waiting for the muffler to be fixed —   126
In Santa Cruz the ocean carves the coast   125
Inside the barren room   159
Inside the storm   49
In the small bed   104
In the still green September   149
I open my book   78
I open my mouth to speak —   81
I open the door and white   164
I placed the sleeping children   9
I slide through the wave —   197
It is easy to leave   66
It is May and I am   79
I wanted hardness when I met him.   74
I watch him walk the long block to the *shul*   194
I will not speak   90
I will wear black   69
jangled in his pocket   183
Just as I get into bed at midnight   162

Just as they were about to be divorced   12
kept wondering   35
kissing your neck.   50
knowing you need to be   97
let's shake loose the fall   88
Light in the heavy hospital bed, so light   192
Little girl scared   185
Love allows   16
Love finds a place   5
Mother O Mother, it was so odd   29
My arms cannot lift your dying   57
My son's shadow stretches out   152
Never wake a sleeping child   193
Next to my mother's bed she kept   103
Nights he sleeps away from home   65
No matter how many   143
None of the men spoke after Beth entered the car.   118
Of all the sweet turnings   181
One day each year the earth cracks open.   45
one day we took turns   96
One white crane lifts from the field   77
Outside my window birds call   202
planting bulbs together in fall   15
Reaching for you this morning   22
Rich is   138
Scatter my ashes in my garden   80
Sharing a joke   33
Shaving his neck I am girl again   153
She opens the window;   63
She who knows   30
Shirtless on the first day of summer   169
Solomon chose an understanding heart.   195
Someday, my son, may you   25
some trip on the tongue   187
speaking to you (my darling)   6
Standing in the doorway, afraid   137
Still at night   73
Stopped at a light, I see my son's babysitter   32
Summoned from sleep   20

Sunset at our backs — 198
suspended from   129
That winter on the farm I watched   165
The big woman   44
The day we left the mountain   130
The day you discover your fingers   24
The deer head mounted on the wall caught me   168
The first holiday after the divorce, Jack sent us gifts.   107
The first time he came inside me   179
The hotel faces the Old City   160
Their glance defines my universe.   23
The last of seven cygnets — tawny thing   188
The muffled cadence of your voice   151
There are times I pause   75
There he sat: Eros   3
the way I keep shaking the milk   95
This house is old. It is not plumb.   199
This storm reminds me of another. Years ago   142
Toss a stone in the water and circles spread across the.   123
Tossed in a low bin of a dusty shop   43
Two months after we sell the Beech Street house   200
We are in a museum, alone.   51
We are young together   58
We finally got around to planting sunflowers   134
We grew up so close   167
We had time only for a brief walk   87
we have warmed   52
We leave this life with what is   204
Well I remember   145
We should have stayed   89
We tied the line   40
We touch by accident   7
We were poor, but never broke.   108
What is this period of time,   60
When a new house blocked the trees   99
When he sleeps with a woman   178
When I conceived you   19
When I finally could sew his damaged clothes   55

When I reach the schoolyard   61
When I think of the waters of childhood, the river   113
when my hair was cut straight across my brow   28
When the storm blew down the tallest tree I could see   53
When we arrive   203
Women will fall open before him   177
Yellow hankies   156
You bring me back   133
You call from a phone booth in Jerusalem   161
You can squander the hour you've saved   150
You know about the heat   116
You lay me on the table   166
You like a man's song   46
Your face feeds at my breast.   18
your hair   91

Acknowledgments

I am grateful to the publishers of my books:
Karl Kulikowski of Gusto Press for *How Odd This Ritual of Harmony* (1981)
Emmet Dingley of Kendall/Hunt Publications for *Ask the Dreamer Where Night Begins* (1986)
George Wallace of Birnham Wood Graphics for *The River* (1990)
Sandra Martz of Papier-Mache Press for *Wetlands* (1993)
John Ellsworth of Eighth Moon Press for *When the Light Falls Short of the Dream* (1998)
Gerald Etra of Whittier Publications, Inc. for *Make Your Way Across This Bridge: New & Selected Writings* (2003)

Thank you to the editors of the following magazines and anthologies for publishing works included in this book: *Nassau Review, Chrysalis, Esprit: A Humanities Magazine, Long Island Quarterly, Hiram Poetry Review, Hawaii Pacific Review, Xanadu: A Literary Journal, Poetica: Reflection of Jewish Thought, Earth's Daughters, Womansmith, The Mickle Street Review, Manhattan Poetry Review, The Fire Island Tide, Infinity Magazine, Live Poets, The Long Islander, The Northport Journal, SCREE, Shooting Star Review, The Sow's Ear, BARK, A, Wordsmith, Calliopes Corner, Skylark, Thirteen, Verve, Laughing Unicorn, Luz en Arte y Literatura, Labyris: A Feminist Arts Journal, Response: A Contemporary Jewish Review, Newsletter Inago, Ripples: New York Marine Education Association, Milkweed Chronicle, San Fernando Poetry Journal, New York Birders, Vintage '45, Waterways, Sandsounds, poetrybay.com, Circus Maximus, nycbigcitylit.com, Footsteps Magazine*

"Stopped at a Light," "slender reed": *I Name Myself Daughter and It Is Good*, Ed. Margaret Honton (Sophia Books, 1981)
"Eros and Civilization," "Morning Warmth": *Island Women*, Ed. Karen Donovan (Women Writers Alliance, 1984)

"Secret Passages," "Torn Pictures," "Dark Pages": *The Poet's Job: To Go Too Far*, Ed. Margaret Honton (Sophia Books, 1985)

"Raining Leaves," "Post Humus": *Raining Leaves,* Ed. Maxwell Corydon Wheat, Jr. (The Great South Bay Cooperative, 1986)

"Post Humus": *When I Am an Old Woman I Shall Wear Purple*, Ed. Sandra Martz (Papier-Mache Press, 1987)

"Men Against the Sky": *Anthology of Magazine Verse & Year book of American Poetry*, Ed. Alan F. Pater (Monitor Book Company, 1988)

"Harbor Island": *American Fiction 88*, Ed. Michael C. White and Alan Davis (Wesley Press, 1988)

"Found Money": *If I Had a Hammer: Women's Work in Poetry, Fiction, and Photographs*, Ed. Sandra Martz (Papier-Mache Press, 1990)

"Torn Pictures": *The Tie That Binds: Fathers & Daughters/ Mothers & Sons*, Ed. Sandra Martz (Papier-Mache Press, 1992)

"Driving Across the Texas Night": *Fine China: Twenty Years of Earth's Daughters* (Earth's Daughters, 1993)

"Calling Up the Moon": *New Covenant: Poems by Long Island Poets for the Clinton Administration*, Ed. George Wallace (Birnham Wood Graphics, 1993)

"Post Humus": *Death: The Trip of a Lifetime*, Greg Palmer (Harper, 1993)

"Makani": *Witnessing Earth*, Ed. Georgette Perry (Catamount Press, 1994)

"Bread": *In Autumn: An Anthology of Long Island Poets*, Ed. George Wallace (Birnham Wood Graphics, 1994)

"Found Money": *Family: A Celebration*, Ed. Margaret Campbell (Peterson's 1995)

"Last Morning in Jerusalem": *Twelve Gates to the City: Spiritual Views on the Journey from Thirty Authors*, Ed. Carol S. Lawson (Chrysalis Books, 1996)

"Post Humus," "Old Habits Die Hard": *Dying: A Book of Comfort*, Ed. Pat McNees (GuildAmerica, 1996)

"The River," "I have touched," "Marvelous Beast," "No," "You Bring Me Back": *Passionate Hearts: The Poetry of Sexual Love*, Ed. Wendy Maltz (New World Library, 1996)

"The Comfort of Time Zones": *The Practice of Peace*, Ed. Judith Rafaela and Nancy Fay (Sherman Asher Publishing, 1998)

"Post Humus": *Among Ants Between Bees*, Ed. Peter McFarlane and Lisa Temple (MacMillan, 1998)

"Dark Pages," "Beware of Lovers," "Gifts" (longer version): *Rape, Incest, Battery: Women Writing Out the Pain*, Ed. Miriam Kalman Harris (TCU Press, 2000)

"My Father's Coins": *Literary Review*, Ed. Joan Magiet (Performance Poets Association, 2000)

"The Lesson": *Not Child's Play*, Ed. Risa Shaw (Lunchbox Press, 2000)

"Turnings": *Literary Review*, Ed. Cliff Bleidner (Performance Poets Association, 2001)

"Lineaments of Desire," "I woke up," "Laughing Thoroughbreds": *Intimate Kisses: The Poetry of Sexual Pleasure*, Ed. Wendy Maltz (New World Library, 2001)

"Fools Rush In" as "Only Fools Rush In": *Touched by Eros*, Ed. George Held (Live Poets Society, 2002)

"The Words," "The Last Tear": *We Used To Be Wives: Divorce Unveiled Through Poetry*, Ed. Jane Butkin Roth (Fithian Press, 2002)

"Post Humus": *Snapshots*, Ed. Julie A. Schumacher (Perfection Learning, 2002)

"Talisman": *The Gift of the Rose*, Ed. Cheryl Carter (Forthcoming)

The following works have been selected for special recognition:

"Eros and Civilization": C. W. Post Poetry Center (1979)

"Living with a Poet": Irma Rhodes Award, The Shelley Society of New York (1983)

"The Big Woman": Long Island Poetry Collective PoemCard (1984)

"Tuesday": First Prize, Peninsula Public Library (1986)

"Harbor Island": *American Fiction 88* (Wesley Press, 1988), Judge: Raymond Carver

"I Can't Believe the Moon": First Prize, *Xanadu: A Literary Journal* (1988)

"Men Against the Sky": *Anthology of Magazine Verse & Yearbook of American Poetry*, Ed. Alan F. Pater (Monitor Book Company, 1988)

"The Wonders of Infinite Smallness": Passaic County Community College Poetry Center (1989)

"McKeever's Hill": *Nassau Review* Poetry Award (1991)

"Post Humus": Read on PBS series *Death: The Trip of a Lifetime*, Greg Palmer (1993)

"Fall Back": Long Island Poetry Collective PoemCard (1997)

"Post Humus": August poem on *When I Am an Old Woman I Shall Wear Purple* calendar, Ed. Sandra Martz (Papier-Mache Press, 1997)

"Fools Rush In": First Prize, Long Island Poetry Collective, Judge: Myra Shapiro (2000)

"Long Beach": First Place, Long Island Waters, The Lake Ronkonkoma Historical Society (2002)

"The Price": First Place, Flora and Fauna, The Lake Ronkonkoma Historical Society (2002)

"Nothing Broke," "Post Humus," "Living with a Poet": Performed by the Poetry Repertory Theater, Scripted and Directed by Susan Melchoir (2000-2003)